DOUBLE HELIX

CONTENTS

This book started into being when my mother died. Sybil had been working, that morning, on her memoirs and I arrived the next day to find them still on the dining table, where she had been sorting them, the chapters tied into neat bundles with a covering note to say that they were now complete. I had sent her a few spring branches—pussy-willow, larch, chestnut—to mark my birthday, and they were in a jar on the table, fully out.

For several years, I carried the bundles from house to house, not opening them and afraid to. It was only when my husband was ill that the courage came to me, and as I read her memoirs I became possessed by astonishment at the way a simple language of natural signs can survive the changing generations and acquire meanings which everyday language seldom embodies. I think that 'poetry' has its root in such signs. In all the individuality of its cultural incarnations, it represents something shared by all human beings. The individuality of a poem may itself be a metaphor for the way universal experiences come to us through, not in spite of, individual responses and thoughts.

Trying to cross the cultural gaps between myself and my mother, myself and my grandmother, and finding everywhere in the memoirs and in family documents evidence of other such gaps, I found it all the more moving that these signs can be shared. Not only that, they seem to be connected with our most vital moments. Sybil's memories of a repressive and isolated Victorian and Edwardian childhood are pierced through by a language of natural signs which is still real for us within our quite different set of conventions.

The documentary core of this book—memoirs, letters, photographs, drawings—represents for me a separate reality (like that of everyday life) which I didn't want to absorb into the poems. Instead, they serve to enforce an effort of 'translation', the idea of which is central to this book. It is ironic that our adaptability is precisely what makes us, too often, strangers to one another—strangers, as it were, to ourselves as we might have been. So the 'helix' of the title

9

refers not only to the spiral of DNA but also to tensions between past and present, man and woman, convention and expression and, most crucially, to another creative tension—that of two lives on either side of a text.

Anne Cluysenaar
Woodend, 10 May 1982

FAMILY VOICES

Thomas Hewat

Bank Manager, Dublin. Father of George.

George Hewat (George)

Colonel in K.O.S.B.'s. Spent many years in India. His first wife died in childbirth, having given him Dora and Francie. His second wife was a cousin, also Hewat, and she gave him my mother Sybil, Michael and Monica. Other children died young in both marriages.

Dora Hewat (Dora, in this text, or 'Doe')

George's second wife, Sybil's mother. She was especially close to her sister Nell, to whom she wrote the few intimate letters that survive. Letters written to Nell during her final breakdown were destroyed by the family before posting. She was sent away to mental homes and spent the rest of her life in care, outliving George by many years.

Sybil Hewat (Sybil)

Eldest child of Dora and George, my mother. She married the Belgian painter John Cluysenaar. She painted professionally but stopped after marriage. Her memoirs were written for me to read, but with the possibility of publication in mind.

Michael Hewat (Michael, or 'Boy')

Sybil's brother. He was killed near Givenchy, March 1915.

'To keep alive the wonder of suffering
You have been metamorphosed into me'—

Anna Akhmatova, Summer 1915.

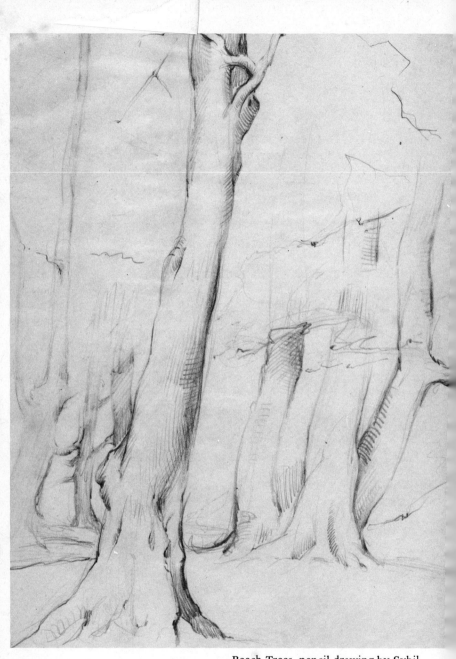

Beech Trees, pencil drawing by Sybil

14

PRINTS LAID DOWN

*   *   *

A dangerous road: many people,
including friends of ours, have died
somewhere along these bends
above the heavenly valley
whose dips and rises, never mind
how well we walk them,
remain the mysterious features
of a dream, disposed by chance
in eternally changing beauty,
corn, shadow, snow-patch, copse, wall,
lemon and dark, furred, smooth, roads hidden.

Before we married, I used to pass
on my way south, your warnings
warm in my ear, but driving fast.
Now, I drive slowly, to work,
taking more care for both our sakes.
This morning, as my favourite bend
brought Wortley into sight, close
round its church and the pub that
we drank at (testing for rumours
of a place like the one we found),
I hear myself speak: 'I wouldn't mind
if I got killed along here.'
An Irish thought, you'll say,
if not too shocked to joke me.
And it's fanciful, too,
if I meant my body would stay here.
Not sure what I had in mind,
I do know that behind the message
lies a way of life whose voice,
newly mine, was always the speech
of those who have somewhere to live.
Our local church handbook tells
how work on the Old Woodhead Tunnel
brought 'terrible accidents', and the dead
left, often, no more than a nickname,

an accent and an age for the vicar's records.
But those men, buried out of sight
round the valley's turn, had their own
chances, unknown to their loving ones.
Like this, unknown to you. Tonight,
making light of it, I know I'll turn
the memory to thankful praise
of your love, even more of yourself
and of all who, like you, can love—
though beyond that, as you know without saying,
it spells a more lonely message: 'the end
of the beginning', and also a victory!
One I think everyone hopes for.

Against the sun, on my way home,
I drive entranced by these white fields
dipping, rising to sombre hills.
Near the roadway, a few sheep
graze, swaddled in light,
and beeches mass to a veined amber.
Safe in the car, struck only by
a dangerous doubt, I hear the voice again—
it is a day for voices—'But others
see this the same way', the beauty, the meaning of matter,
'and who do you want to speak to, but others?'

*   *   *   *

MEMOIRS OF SYBIL HEWAT

Looking Backward

I have often wished that I myself could know more about my
ancestors—about their real feelings, habits and daily life as well
as about their looks, their dress, and the more obvious facts
of their existence. It is easy to find superficial trace of two
or three generations, but I feel sure that one would discover
much further back unexpected traits of one's own which ori-
ginated with them and which they would be astonished, were

16

such a thing possible, to recognize. And is it so impossible, seeing that scientists have arrived at showing us that Time as such does not exist (and I must believe them for my mind refuses to grasp the fact if left to itself!). If for example men were able to visit Mars, a distance of X miles at X miles per hour, it would occupy so many hours, days & years (which in fact only exist as one calculates on this planet) and they would on their return to earth find that those days and years had in fact elapsed; their children would be grown up—possibly even their grandchildren—and all the inevitable changes would have taken place. Yet I am encouraged to think that they would have spent a happy weekend or so whereas their families would have followed the calendar as we know it, and aged accordingly! Be that as it may, it seems conceivable that some day one might be able to look back freely, putting aside Time as we still understand it, and get to know at close quarters those ancestor of ours. Maybe a fairytale! but an intriguing prospect; and who at the present time (with telephone, television and such daily conveniences taken for granted, not to mention discoveries of Science undreamed of in even a quite recent past when they would have been smiled upon as fantastic imaginings of the Irresponsible)—who can affirm with any certitude that such are impossible dreams. A sense of humour opens up possibilities, and one can imagine meetings and interviews humorous and dramatic, happy or alarming for both ancestors and descendants faced with this phenomenon! But no doubt they would come to look upon it all as natural in the same way that we show little or no surprise at seeing and hearing on screens at home what is at the same moment happening beyond sight in other parts of the Globe—even hearing human voices from Space; voices possibly of friends or relatives until lately beside us in our houses, a part of everyday life. Within far less than my lifetime one's only comment would have been 'mad'.

* * * *

17

In time-lapse, falling, rising,
our lives create, again and again,
for the world, moments of self-knowing.
Joy or sorrow, for all the difference matters,
tears the unique solitary fabric
from which consciousness flows beyond,
wave on wave—our million biographies
obliterated, footprints at high tide.

As, without silence, speech is nothing,
so my love for you is nothing without this nothing.
You are what will never be again, a sentence
made out of the world to tell me love.
And love, even as it wavers, is enough
to hold sacred the meanings of life,
faults, failures, conditions, coincidences,
ludicrous courageous details to which we witness
through our only forever.
                              In the perfect republic,
Milosz says, 'they walk contemplating
the holy word: Is—so early in the morning
that the sun has barely made it through the dense maples'.
Here, the sun hardly makes it at all, the rain
mildews, day after summer day, our bank of dogroses—
the roses of such true, wild, simple love
that poets dare no longer mention them!
All the same, some ignoramus who never heard
of poetry, is walking down there, so early,
by the stream, and stops to look, thinking himself alone,
while his black dog pursues something more interesting.
Thoughts that are part of my world—as are mine
of his—pass silently on with his hunched figure
into the drizzle: he crosses the bridge out of sight.
The moment can never be otherwise. Together
we rest in it, it is a footprint
fossilized on a shore, the silt
of words happening to drift this way
with the obliterating tide.
                              So matter, sometimes,
sees itself, as it rises and falls,

and leaves a record of what is anyway immortal.
'If not I, then someone else,' wrote Milosz,
'would be walking here, trying to understand . . .
I was not necessary.' The unnecessary poet,
the man with the dog, are ciphers, the conversation
of matter with itself, in which I is truly another.

And who needs to be necessary, except to those
whose love is witness? It is enough
to recognize, to be recognized, and the rest
is the price of love, a small price even.
I think so, and watch the impossible thought
like a wave, now white, now black,
travel away, beyond and over us.

* * * *

MEMOIRS OF SYBIL HEWAT

Beginnings

My father had ten children. Four daughters now survive, and only five children lived beyond babyhood, the only surviving boy being killed in action in 1915.

His first wife was very young (about twenty two I think) when they married. He was stationed for a time in India and later usually in Britain. Army life in India was very primitive in those days, and must in some ways have been an alarming experience for her, coming as she did from away down in Cornwall. As a young wife she was more than once left alone with native servants even when she was expecting a baby while my father was on shooting expeditions; and she once confided to her sister-in-law Jessie, who she found understanding and sympathetic, her dread of having another child. In those days in England at any rate, most people were very unenlightened about these things and birth control except in medical circles was scarcely mentioned. She had two girls: six years between the eldest, Dora, and Francie, who came after two boys who

19

died in infancy. She did have another son after confiding her fears to her sister-in-law—it was almost as if she had a presentiment for she died at his birth, and though apparently a strong baby he only survived a few months.

So that my father, as quite a young man, found himself with two little girls of ten and four. I am indebted to Aunt Jessie for these glimpses of the early days, for she was fond of both my father's wives. Being in the army, he could not cope with the situation by himself and so his wife's sister Minna took the job, and being a typical old-maid she coddled and fussed over those two children, wrapped them up in mufflers to 'keep out the cold air', so that to my eldest sister this temporary regime remains a nightmare. It did not suit my father either; he needed a wife at home. He had a large family of cousins living just outside London, and apparently visited them fairly frequently. Their mother was a first cousin of his own (though the two generations were in age very far apart) and the daughters I imagine took a romantic interest in this very handsome young widower and his two little girls, and from the brood he chose Dora, nicknamed Dot or Doe by her brothers and sisters, and she consented to marry him. She was genuinely fond of him I think. And probably at that time she genuinely longed to be a Mother to the two girls. My mother's home, St. Cuthberts, was a large Victorian house within sight of the Crystal Palace (a great landmark to Londoners at that epoch) and I think the household is worth describing if only briefly. I was taken there from time to time, and remember certain impressions of those early visits very clearly (without the aid of family groups, which show a remarkably handsome elderly couple surrounded by eight of their sons and daughters).

My grandmother ruled the household with a strong will for order and a great capacity for management. Her husband was a kindly bearded figure whose voice was seldom raised—much more easy going than she was but from all accounts nervous and not very strong.

My memories of the old house are connected with a strong smell of pitch pine (added doubtless to much polish) with which the stairway and the large square hall were covered. This smell met one when, after pealing a heavy door bell, one

The Hewat Girls

Alice

Ethel   Eliza (m. Charles Pearson)   Dora (m. George Hewat)

Nell

came into the hall. Further at the top of the stairs to the basement one was met by a peculiarly musty smell which I recognized on successive visits over 25 years of my existence and connect with this house though there were sometimes many years' interval between my visits. In the basement there was a huge store cupboard or room opened only by my grandmother who kept a large bunch of keys dangling at her waist for this purpose when she interviewed the cook and handed out the daily essentials. One used the stairs to the basement frequently, as there was, apart from the servants' quarters, a large square room called the gunroom, through which one could pass by a french window into the gardens, where one found a terrace with wide steps leading to lawns, and further into 'the wilderness', a wild part given over to woodland and covered in spring with wild anemones, primroses and daffodils. A high wooden paling separated all this from a quiet road beyond, and as there was little or no traffic in the surrounding roads one had the sensation of being cut off in a very peaceful and well-run oasis!

The servants were of long-standing, and 'Old Nurse of St. Cuthbert' was a much loved figure, if somewhat formidable to the young, having been wet-nurse to at least one of the family and stayed on in the position of housekeeper. The family lived very much to themselves, seldom travelled or visited, and were held by unquestioned rules at home. There is a letter amongst a bundle I have, written by my mother, Dora, as a small girl to her mother, 4 pages obviously written entirely by herself with many scratchings out, which shows how from early days 'Mamma' liked to keep a personal contact with the children. This letter was written to her mother on a visit to the sea with Nell and the baby Ethel. Claude and she had been playing together—and she said she 'was eating strawberries all the time' that she was writing. Uncle John of Bracknell had been inspecting Claude's rod, 'and gave him a shilling to buy hooks and lines'.

Another letter from about this date (1869) is to Dora from her grandmother in Edinburgh. 'My dear little Dora; I shall be quite happy to have you at Murcheston, and was very much pleased to get your letter this morning. Perhaps I might have room for dear little Nellie also, as I am going to send Alice away to Elie because do you know she goes to the Biscuit tin and takes out the biscuits without ever asking my permission to do so . . . I did ask your sister Eliza to come and stay with me, but she has never troubled herself to say if she was to come—So it will be better for her to go away at once to Elie, and enjoy the sea side. Murcheston will be too quiet for her now she has been to Rome'. From this I gather that my great grandmother was not a very easy going old lady, and that the ways of the younger generation did not always come up to her standards of behaviour! Also that as the family grew up the elder girls were not so willing to be dictated to in the details of everyday existence! 'Grayhurst', the letter continues, 'was here all last Saturday and spent the whole day beside me, as Alice and the Aunts were all out. He is such a good boy and so happy at school. He sometimes brings one of his companions across with him, and then they get a bit of Rock. We are all longing to see the dear little sister'. It seems to me curious that the old lady should have voiced complaints about her elder sister to Dora who in 1869 was a very small girl; but I daresay that the idea was that the reproof would get round to Eliza and Alice without the necessity of writing a letter to each of them!

To go back to St. Cuthbert's: the house was always open to any connections of the family, and they were numerous and particularly united as were so many Scottish families—the Clan spirit, in fact. I was told that the boys were never otherwise allowed to bring back friends to the house; or at any rate such a procedure was not smiled upon and could only be done very judiciously and with due warning. Probably only likely admirers of the girls were allowed? If I seem to criticize I do so with diffidence, for I have an immense respect for that older generation in spite of considerable amusement at times over conventions and habits, and am well aware that I can only describe them as they have appeared to me with memory and a few old letters to guide me. They did not exteriorize, and it would be difficult to get past very well-ordered appearances. That they were good class was accepted without question, and didn't interest them any more than they were interested in general in what is termed 'Society'. It is true that later, when the eldest daughter Eliza came into touch, because of her husband's position, with most politically important people both in England and Scotland, the interests of the family seem to have widened in this respect. One of the sons, Grayhurst ('Gar' to the family) worked in a city Bank, and often went by the name of 'Banker'; Claude my mother's favourite brother tea-planted in Ceylon till he died shortly before she married. And the third, Richard, ran away to sea, sowing his wild oats in proverbial fashion, finally settling within sight of the waves he loved on an estuary on the South Coast where he owned a yacht 'The Wild Cat'. He was the most colourful of the brothers, though seldom heard of. I remember him as Uncle Dick—a giant of a man, bearded, and with startlingly blue laughing eyes under wide brows. He was somewhat suspicious of the family but very kindly. He must have lived a lonely life in a way. I think he drank more than was generally admitted and possibly more than was good for him as I've heard vague tales of empty bottles which periodically had to be discreetly disposed of. He looked a very fine figure, very much of a gentleman though at that time there was no need to underline the fact, taking it for granted as obvious. When he died, when I was scarcely grown up, the yacht was left to the two men who sailed it for him and with whom he had spent so many carefree days. They thought the world of him and I believe the Cat sailed for many years though I don't know her final fate and possibly she may still be cared for and sea-worthy.

The girls of the family were carefully brought up at home and at a school run by an old friend of the family. Dora and Nell were sent together to Bonn which was a marvellous experience for them, and they spoke German well and never forgot certain little phrases which they often used. They were all taken in turns fairly frequently to the theatre in London, where several seats were reserved at the Haymarket in the front row of the dress circle for the first night of every new production there. On these occasions little bottles of port-wine were provided as 'sustenance', each member of the expedition being armed with one in which a little tube was set so that behind a handkerchief the liquid could be discreetly partaken of. The same procedure followed when they went up as happened sometimes to hear a particular debate or speech in the House of Lords. Grandpapa must have been emotional, as it is related that he fainted with horror on one occasion during Henry Irving's performance of 'The Bells'.

Nell was gay and friendly, and loved to go and stay on visits with friends and relatives whenever she got the chance. She told me that once when she was having a good time it was abruptly curtailed by a post card from 'Mamma' on which she read simply 'chapter so & so, verse so & so'. When she looked this up in her bible (which of course she had with her) she found 'Remove thy foot from thy neighbour's doorstep, lest he weary of thee and so hate thee.' Needless to say there was nothing to do but scuttle home.

All the girls in turn were sent to suitable establishments abroad to be 'finished'—well chaperoned one may be sure, and if the Parents knew more of life in general than was apparent they would not have admitted it to the girls who were, until they married, kept extremely sheltered and innocent (or should I say ignorant?) even for that period. As the older girls found husbands they kept their newly-found experience and knowledge to themselves, and only spoke of married life and children in a strictly drawing-room fashion. 'Mamma' explained nothing of the mysteries of sex even when they married. Such things were simply not spoken of and I seriously think only thought of in the dark under the comforting cover of adequate bed clothes. A spade was never called a spade, and conversation at home, except perhaps childishly simple chatter between the girls, seems to have left out of the ruling the simple facts of life and therefore many of the essential truths.

So it was that when my mother married, although getting on for thirty, she unbelievably knew absolutely nothing of what is now-a-days fairly freely discussed amongst the young, or at any rate the knowledge is to be had for the asking, surely a very much wiser and more healthy outlook even if exaggerated—the swing of the pendulum.

What my mother expected is hard to imagine except that babies were sent by God. Marriage was to her an adventure in an imaginary world; an utterly unexpected experience and in all probability she was not let down lightly. Her sister in law, Jessie, to whom I am indebted for these details, told me that she personally had been shocked by the atmosphere she found when she spent a few days with the newly married couple. She considered that my mother should never have been asked to face it. She was plunged into the home and atmosphere of the first wife with nothing changed and photos of her every-where—There were the old servants to be contended with,

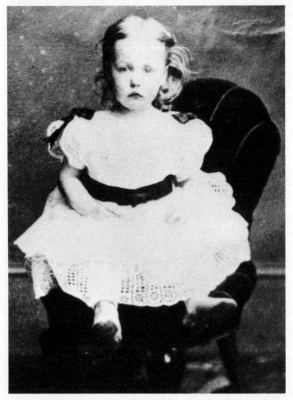

Dora Hewat, 1864

and they were violently resentful of her advent which they regarded as an intrusion, and their antagonism surprised and horrified my mother. She had had no experience of running a house and was living under impossible conditions which, had my father been sensitive to such things, should never have existed. He had a kind, generous and easy-going disposition and a quick Irish temper, and I suppose I might say that he was not concerned with unexpected situations which connected in no way with his knowledge of regimental discipline. Jessie,

26

who had married my father's eldest brother, probably saw things in a fairly detached way, being thorough-going, practical and down-to-earth in contrast to the family into which she had married, where Irish traits were very much in evidence. A few weeks after her visit the inevitable happened, a bad nervous breakdown from which my mother only recovered some months later. When she came back from the nursing home to normal life it was under happier conditions; new maids and a brighter home, and she had a chance of getting to know the two little daughters as well as riding and driving about the country with my father. The regiment was soon ordered to India and she went out with him leaving the two little girls in Aunt Minna's charge at home.

*   *   *   *

LETTER FROM THOMAS HEWAT TO HIS SON, GEORGE

Monkstown. [Dublin]
1st August, 1869.

My dear George,
   I have not heard of your return to London, but I presume you got back there on Thursday, and I hope you found what I sent for you to Broad Street, and got all things in order for Sandhurst, where I trust this may find you at an early hour tomorrow forenoon—You will find it a good rule through life to guard against accidents by being always in time in whatever you have to do, and I trust you have observed this rule by deciding to go down in the forenoon so as to reach Sandhurst early, whoever has gone with you, and I shall be glad to hear from you soon to tell me how you are circumstanced, and how you like Sandhurst and your companions there.—A great deal depends on yourself, and your respectability and success in after life will be greatly affected by your conduct and the character you earn for yourself while at Sandhurst.—It is the trial of your steadiness and industry and general conduct, and your first object every day is to keep steadily in view the importance of every step you gain. Let your first object be to

attend to the duties of religion, and after that to take advantage of the opportunities for Study and for instruction which you will have at the College—Aim at pleasing the Masters and all the ruling Authorities at the college and while you make yourself agreeable to your companions by a frank manner and gentleman-like conduct at all times and towards all, you should be careful to guard against too great intimacy with any until you fully understand their character, and satisfy yourself that you will derive improvement and advantage from their acquaintance, and associate as much as possible with those who like yourself aim at improvement, and are steady and careful in their character and habits—and don't allow yourself to grumble or to be dissatisfied with any of the rules or regulations, or managements of the institution.—Be assured that the Authorities know by experience what is best, and that all persons in charge or having authority there must be supported in the management of the details, so that you should not join in any discontents exhibited by any ill conditioned young men, but use all the influence you may possess amongst your companions, in promoting good order, and harmony amongst them and in the institution generally.—You will be there only a short time, a year, or a year and a half, at most, and it will be a great satisfaction to you through life to look back on that period as well and advantageously spent, and as being the period in which you acquired the information and the qualifications, and the character that will make you respected and happy and promote your advancement in life.—Small matters accumulate and mount up to large and important, so that you should consider every little thing to have its own amount of influence, and you should therefore get into the habit of doing everything carefully and well, and of reflecting upon what you have in mind so as to derive all the benefit possible from all you are engaged in every day you live.—You have seen how closely I have applied myself to the duties of my station in life, and your advantages now are infinitely greater than any I enjoyed or had within my reach at your age, and if you throw these away, or do not make the best use of them, you will have reason to regret it as long as you live.

I do not know that I can say more to influence you for good, as you must now act in every thing on your own judgement, according to the circumstances in which you may be placed, but if you study to act as your best friends would wish you, and pray to God for guidance in all your ways, you will never go far wrong.—

I should remind you to be very careful never to incur debt. You will have about D.2. with you according to the regulations, and you will receive your regular allowance of 2/6 a week or more according to your rank and position at the College and that should be quite enough for all your wants there—and you should want nothing until you come home at Christmas that you have not money to pay for, and you should not allow any thing to tempt you to borrow money or to buy any thing on credit, and be very careful of any tradesmen or others who may endeavour to tempt you to do any thing of the kind, and avoid the society of any young men you see inclined to be *idle* or *expensive*, or *selfindulgent* in any way, and cultivate that of those who are steady, industrious, moderate and self-denying, for these are they who are laying the foundation for future respectability and success in life.—You will not always have me to supply your wants, and until you are able to fend for yourself you should study to make your wants as few as possible, but be careful in your dress and always cleanly and neat in your person and habits, and quietly frank and agreeable in your manner to all, and ready to oblige whenever you have opportunity, or are called upon—and by observing what I have tried to point out you will I am sure derive great advantage from the training you will receive at Sandhurst. We will expect to hear from you frequently, and will always be glad to hear all your news but bear in mind that a little written care-fully and well will be of greater advantage to yourself than volumes of careless and hurried writing or work of any kind. —With all my best wishes, I remain always your very affectionate
Thomas Hewat

*   *   *   *

George in uniform

He took his father's advice. Carefully and well
he censored the news of life, both to others
and to himself.
                    His dress sword meets earth
at a determined angle, though the tip
dips into shadow. He chose his wives
for a sensitive weakness he made sure to lack.
Death and madness removed them: through childbirth,
childloss. It must have seemed that all acts
of creation were dangerous. He had no use
for women's nature-babble, the maintenance
of long-distance affection. And in fact their words
were unfit for disaster. They died or broke down
in silence, their tears like their deeper joys
'private' to the end, their intimate letters
burnt by a sensible household as signs of madness.
The decorous cry, art's double helix,
was not in their tradition.
                         Refusing to have madness
home, in the shape of his wife, he wasted away
to die quiet, military language likewise
not to the purpose. Only that other helix
of live tissue continues their argument,
joining with other voices, linking and sharing
ancient opposing wisdoms to new purposes.
Which have changed little, though their contexts change.

In the photo, his balance is assured by one foot
and that useless sword. The other foot
hesitates, as in life, between stance and step.

                    *   *   *   *

31

Dora, 1879

18 Blackford Road [Edinburgh]
Sunday afternoon, Feb. 9, 1890

My dearest Nell—the other 2 sheets are just a pretence. What I really want to tell you about are my *hunting* experiences at Lochmalen.

Fancy me hunting! and, oh, my dear *'wot larx'*—You have no conception of the excitingness of it. I really did not dream of doing such a thing when I went to Mayfield—for one thing it had never occurred to me that George would take me. The afternoon I arrived at Lochmalen we went out for a ride—& the next morning George said 'Well, are you coming to the meet today?' He did not atall *press* me to go—in fact he seemed a little uncertain about it—& Minna evidently was nervous. She thought it would be so dreadful if anything happened to me. George kept saying 'Well, you know, if you like to go I can depend upon the *horses*—they won't stop at anything', and so on. Of course I didn't exactly like to *say* I could depend upon sticking on, tho' I thought I could. Then another objection of George's was that I had a soft hat wh. he said was quite unsafe. I *certainly* should never have gone atall had it not been that I had gone jumping the previous week on the filly with Hunter and Miss Tim, & so I really thought I shd. be all right & at last I just said decidedly I would go. At wh. I think George was in reality rather pleased.

I can assure you I found no reason to repent my decision. I shd. have been very sorry if I hadn't gone. When I came down dressed, I found G. had arranged to take his man with his second horse. 'And then', he said, 'you can just come back with Bell, or he will show you the way along the roads'. This was rather a relief to my mind, I felt so dreadfully afraid of being in George's way. So off we started at 10 o'c. and rode to the Meet. George introduced me to two or three people. There were 4 ladies I think beside myself. Of course when they asked me things I just said I knew nothing about hunting. 'Oh no', George said, 'and my cousin is not going to hunt today.' So we all rode off & they began looking for a fox & drawing the different covers. They were all very unsuccessful & at last

33

we got quite up into the hills. Of course all the time we were not on roads & sometimes we went pretty fast & sometimes we came to jumps. After 2 or 3 of these George remarked to me 'Dear me, why, you're all right—Why didn't you say so before' —!—After we had been out a couple of hours he changed his horse & when he came up to me again I found he had sent Bell home with his grey without further ado. So I felt I was fairly launched, & George made no more proposals of my going home! It was a lovely day & we were out riding for 6 hours, tho' we had no 'run', & G. considered it poor. I enjoyed it very much, & I have thought since it was quite enough for me for a beginning. They started 3 foxes at last, but George and I had our eye on the wrong one, & we lost the hounds. So when we found they had gone off in a different direction we just rode home where we arrived about 4 o'c. & I was not sorry to have some lunch. Of course I knew simply *nothing* about what to do, so I just followed George exactly, & kept close to him, & did whatever he did. I got a great fright by seeing one *very* fat old gent. come off at a hedge—his horse fell—but neither of them seemed any the worse. Another gent: was down in the course of the day.

Next day G. had business in Dumfries, & off he marched with the skirt of my habit, & had a huge leather patch put on the knee, as he said otherwise I shd. be wet thro' in ms. if we were out in rain—he also came back with a parcel of hard, round, black hats under his arm, one of wh: he insisted on my adopting. Next day there was another meet, & he surveyed me with gt. satisfaction when I was mounted, patch, hard hat & all, & said now he felt safer. He is a most amusing fellow, & *so* kind, the idea of his letting me ride his horses in the way he did! This day I ride Moy—we had a run, but were only out for about 2½ hrs—were hunting up on the hills wh. is hard work, & it was '*pooring*' the whole time.

But it was on the Saturday my dear that I so distinguished myself, & *won a brush*! after a run of 16 miles with only one check. It *was* a hard day's work if you like. We mounted at 10 o'c. and dismounted at 6 p.m. and all that time I only had three biscuits! We had two runs—a short one in the morning, & then this tremendous one fr. Lochmalen to Annan—it was *quite* an unusual thing. George told me they seldom get a run

34

of more than 7 or 8 miles. It is so *fearfully* exciting—it takes a lot out of you—how the hounds do tear along when they get the scent—I had no idea they could go so fast—one has to gallop full tilt to keep up. I just followed George & the chestnut carried me most splendidly—never refused anything. I did not know how tired I was until we had stopped running, & George told me we had 13 miles to jog home—the fox was not killed, as he had given them such a splendid run the hounds were whipped off. Oh! how *endless* those 13 miles seemed—& George went about a mile out of the way—it began to *pour* long before we got home, & I simply can't describe to you how tired I was when I slipped from the chestnut at 6 o'c. I could hardly stand! Minna had begun to wonder where on earth we were. Dinner was put off until 8 o'c. & as I had to undress at any rate I just got into bed for 2 hrs. & rested. Never in my life did I enjoy anything so much as the cup of tea Minna brought me after I was between the sheets.

George said I had quite distinguished myself & that *any*one would be tired even if they were accustomed to hunting. I know he did not appear himself till dinner time. I was all right next day, & on Tuesday when they killed in a quarry after a short fast run of about 5 miles, the old huntsman came up to me and asked if I would accept the brush. Of course it was because of Sat: I was *awfully* proud of it really tho' I pretended to G. I didn't like the smell!!

I never enjoyed anything so much in my life as the hunting, & I don't suppose I ever shall. I had a delightful time. George was so kind—& Minna too—she was most good. I do hope you will see something of her. I am sure you wd. like her so much, & she was *so* good to me—coddled me fearfully.

Now I must stop—but before saying Farewell I want just to ask you if you can give me any idea what you gave the servants at Drumsheugh the winter you were there? do try to tell me if you recollect.

I don't know whether you will care about this screed—but I thought I *must* tell you about my experiences, tho' I can't convey to you any idea of how wildly I enjoyed it all. Ever your devoted Doe.

*   *   *   *

35

Dora with her first-born, Sybil. Muree, India, 1894

Letters and memoirs seem to tell me less
than this luminous fossil—so strictly posed,
a band of metal just visible at the neck,
keeping the stance steady—this true image
of a bond neither could afterwards recall.
The details are enigmatic. I peer closely,
deciphering each hair, each youthful wrinkle
in grandmother's smile, the shining lower lip,
soft, surely loving, the large capable hand
on which my mother's fist, clenched in delight,
has left a tender shadow.
                          I read through letters
written to sister, mother at home in England.
She had broken down already, just after marriage,
and soon, before mother was ten, she'd be taken away
to unvisited mental homes, whose names are forgotten.
The letters are those of a woman with few enjoyments,
all of them private, none trivial: a lawn robe
for baby, a view, a puppy, a cool morning garden,
a rare picnic with the husband she hardly mentions.

Scanning this print, left on the alien light
of another country, another century—
Muree, India, 1894—
I recognize, in this way of holding the child
temple to temple at shoulder height, the love
her first-born gave me, forty-two years later.
Forty-two years later still, as I calculate
forward and backward in time, I seek the words
that will pose my feeling.
                          Photographed in rock,
the fragile shapes of our ancestors flow still
on the drift of a tide turned these three million years.
They settled just so, one day, one forgotten moment.
I lay the two prints together.
                          Christmas has passed.
Amongst our cards, no haloed *Mother and Child*
tempts us to sentiments we can't abide by.
Outside, as the year begins, snow falls like silt—
the worst since childhood, for us in our middle age.

The typewriter drops its silt into the silence.
Those hours, and these, in all their details of writing,
of reading, are now invisible fossils that no one
could recall. All the prints are laid down together.

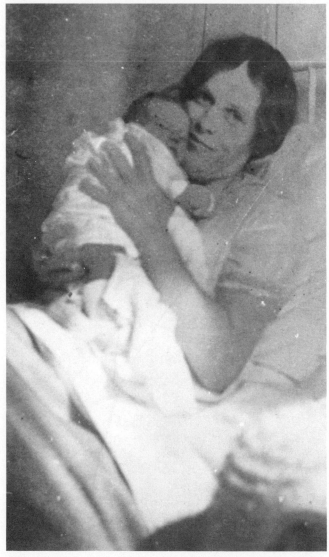

Sybil with her only child, Anne. Brussels, 1936

38

Pindi [India]
Christmas Day, 1894.

My dearest mother,

Many thanks for your letter of 30th. Nov: and to Ethel for her enclosure—also for the Xmas Graphic & various other papers. We get a home mail in this evening—but of course these letters will be posted before it comes.

It was *pouring* with rain yesterday, and the roads were a mass of sticky mud—fortunately one never has to walk in this part of the world! Today it is grey and cold, & altogether most abominable weather—it has been raining too this morning, but looks now as if it might possibly clear up & let us have a glimpse of the sun.

I must not go any further without thanking you very much indeed for your charming Xmas present. I really do think you are getting *very* extravagant!! I like the gowns very much indeed, and am sure they will be most useful. They arrived all right a few days ago—the gowns were rather crushed, but nothing that an iron will not set right again, & it was only the fault of the folding as the box wh. held them was in perfect condition. I think I prefer the peacock blue one *with* the ribbon round the waist, as otherwise one looks so very voluminous. Very many thanks for the lace, & the pretty insertion, & black moiré ribbon.

Nell's too came at the same time. I wonder what made you think of sending Sybil that delightful ball? it is just *the* very thing I was wanting for her! She wakes up always now at about 5.30 a.m. as bright as a button wh: is most undesire-able at that early hour. She always wants to crow & play—so now I hang your ball up on her curtain rod & she lies & plays with it, & knocks it about to her heart's content—& if it does hit her on the nose it is no matter.

Please thank Ethel very much for the extremely pretty little tray—& Aunt Maggie for the jackets for Baby. I will try to write to her soon.

4 p.m. The sun came out this morning after all, & it has turned into a nice bright day. We are coming over tonight to dine with the McArthurs. Mrs McA. is able to sit up now for

dinner, and she went for her first drive today. Moira is three weeks old this afternoon. She is a tiny mite but is filling out a little now. Mrs Becker is also up, but she has not been out yet —her baby is a most *splendid* specimen.

Such an awful thing happened here last Thursday—Colonel Money of the 9th. Bengal Lancers was shot by a man in his own regt. The regt. had been at a Camp of exercise at Muridki, & were just coming back to Pindi. George & I were calling on Mrs Money on Thursday morning, & she was telling him about the regt. railing back fr. camp, & saying how glad she would be to have Col: Money back. A few hours after that he was dead. It has cast quite a gloom over everything. The man who shot him was a bad character & Col: Money had passed him over on that account & not given him his promotion, & this was the way he revenged himself. Isn't it *awful* for poor Mrs Money— & to make matters worse she is left very badly off.

Col: M's body was brought back to Pindi on Friday night, & the funeral was on Saturday—a huge affair—George had to go of course. The next horrible thing will be the public execution of the man—there will be an enormous parade to wh: all the troops have to go.

Sybil's last accomplishment is getting her toes right into her mouth.

Please thank Nell *very* much indeed for sending me the things I wanted. I will write to her next week.

With love to all. Ever yr. loving Dot.

Many thanks to Eliza and Alice for letters—also to Sir Charles for his.

Dora's outline of Sybil's foot dated 7 April 1895

India, dark with rain. A woman was sitting
at a borrowed window. And it was Christmas,
1894.
         Possibly I shall live
to see the hundredth year, 1994.
The mystery of dates!
                           She could not see
her own fate, the years of forsaken madness,
alien in her own country, in sombre houses
where no one is at home. Nor see
her baby's baby, writing at another window
in an England dark with rain. Around us both,
the different and same world, better
and worse. My luck better than hers,
so far, love being the only luck
our sanity needed. But that teasing echo,
1984: it even seems good,
compared to the world our weapons promise.
There, there are still trees, rebellion,
hopes, loves to be broken, a fate.
There, there will be no actions, no failures,
no fate: a sensible emptiness,
world without subjects—worse than insanity.
Where then will be the source of freshness
deep down things, to which the human mind
has access, that song of flowing waters?
What is the good of asking? 2094,
if someone is there to answer, will have its questions—
on earth, or somewhere else, its own weather,
its holy word.
                  Around her, had she known,
the holy Shabd was being heard by a people
whose breasts she did not wish her children to nurse at.
A milk was flowing, that might have saved her.

         *   *   *   *

41

A was the Atom we all loved so well,
B are the Blue eyes of Bonny Sea-bell,
C are the Crows that she gives when she's pleased,
D the 'Don'ts' that she tries to express when she's squeezed,
E the Endearing ways, charming us all,
F little Fat Fingers, which cling lest she fall,
G are the Glances she casts on her cousin,
H are the Howls, wh. she makes by the dozen,
I is her Intellect, sharp as a needle,
J are her 'Jouets' soon broken and feeble,
K are the Kisses she kindly concedes,
L is the Laugh wh. the kisses precedes,
M is the Mouth with lips smiling and red,
N is her Nose, quite retroussé, 'tis said,
O are the Onlookers watching her tub,
P is the Powder, wh. oer her we rub,
Q is the Queen who to rule us is able,
R are the Rabbits she feeds at the stable,
S is the Sleep she takes, peaceful and sound,
T are her little Toes, pink, soft and round,
U is her Uncle, who on her does dote,
V is her Voice, where no harshness I note,
W is her Whole, such a sweet little Pet,
X is the meal she Xpects, but not yet,
Y is the Yellow silk fluff on her head—
Z is too hard—so you'll take it as said.

Duneaves, July 95

Poem written by Dora, Sybil's mother, at Duneaves, 1895

*   *   *   *

Sybil with Anne, June 1937

Kashmir
August 9, 1902

My darling Boy—

I like the nice photo of you and Sybil in the door way at Bella Vista *so* much. It came yesterday. What a pity your donkey moved his head, wasn't it? Sybil's one has come out so beautifully.

I will enclose you another Sunday group, which I did last Sunday, after Uncle Arthur had shaved off his beard. It is not very good. Father is screwing up his eyes so.

Monica is very pleased because she has another little bird's nest. Sunday found it for her a few days ago, there were eggs in it, but two days ago when Monica went she found tiny birds, and she was *so* delighted.

I hope your green finches' nest in the garden will get little birds in it.

This morning Sunday brought me *such* a neat little thing to look at. I wish I could put it into your letter for you to see, but it would all crumble into dust. It is a little spider's nest made of mud, like this , & just about this size. The round thing is a hole—and inside I saw a little spider & some funny little round cocoons, which I suppose are eggs, or contain eggs. It is so neat. The spider had made it in a fold in my tent.

I am so glad you liked Harwood so much—you will have had to leave it by this time I am afraid—

I enclose a note for Cark. With lots of love and kisses to you and Sybil—

Your loving

Mother.

*   *   *   *

44

Rowbury's Hotel, Muree
April 15, 1902

My darling Sybil—

I liked your last letter so much. With the envelope nicely addressed in ink. We have not got our letters yet this week.

How I wish you & Boy & Cark were here with us—it is so nice and we are having lovely fine weather now. Dora & I have been down several times to Spur Cottage, the little house where you were born—and yesterday I gathered you a little bunch of violets from the wood just outside the garden. I wonder if they will have any scent by the time they reach you. When I go down there I wish that you were here and that you were a dear little, tiny, pink baby again! On Sunday we go to the church where you were Christened.

Poor little Monica has had a *very* bad cold in her head, but I am glad to say she is much better now—nearly well again. There are some tiny babies here now, 9 & 10 months old, and she likes them very much indeed—she strokes their faces, & I am always so afraid she will put her fingers in their eyes! She says a lot of new words.

Do you remember your dear little green coat? The one Aunt Nell gave you in York & that you used to wear in the garden at Aldershot—Monica wears it now. She has it for a dressing gown in the morning, and she will wear it in Kashmir—we have got some new pink ribbon for strings for the bonnet. I am going to try to get another little coat made, the same pattern, because I like it so much.

Will you ask Cark if she has the paper pattern of your first little pink pyjamas, because if she has I wish she would send it to me. I shall want to make pyjamas for Monica before she comes home.

You & Boy would like to go about in the woods here, & pick the dear little violets & maiden hair fern. We find great big fir cones too & we bring them home for our fire, they make such a splendid blaze.

We hope Father would be up tomorrow, but I do not think he will be here now till Thursday or Friday. Lots of love & kisses to you and Boy. Ever your loving   Mother.

Edinburgh

After Aldershot, my father's regiment was ordered out to India again, and our parents went out taking the baby Ruth with them. The two elder girls were left with Aunt Minna (their own mother's sister) and Michael and I (accompanied by our governess 'Cark') were offered a home by my mother's sister Eliza and her husband in Edinburgh—a Judge, Privy Councillor and I believe brilliant in his way, one of the most charming of men. She had been young when they married and they had had three sons (the only girl had died). These boys were young men when we two appeared to recreate a nursery atmosphere on the top landing of the very large town house where they lived. Wide steps led up from the pavement of the Square and the door at the top of the steps seemed enormous with its great brass knob, knocker and bell, and as it opened a very small girl was lifted high in the air by two strong arms while a cheery voice said with a laugh 'so this is Sybil'. When I again landed on my feet there was a buzz of talking and my impressions became jumbled, intermingling. Other people came forwards, cold air cut in from the outside till the luggage was safely in the hall with the butler in charge and at last the door was shut. Our luggage, always voluminous in those days, was carried upstairs by the butler and maids and a great deal of talking went on amongst the grown-ups who were anxious to know details of our journey from Cark. We were I think, three and four at the time and very bad travellers. After what seemed an age someone suggested that 'the chicks must be tired', and I was thankful to be carried upstairs and put to bed without more ado.

It was only next day that we explored our new abode. The night nursery was at the end of a long passage with a bath-room quite close, and the day nursery overlooked the gardens of the Square. There were two windows with bars to prevent any possibility of falling out, and window-seats with lids, inside which we could keep our toys. We could sit or stand on these window-seats too and see all that went on below: for we were right on the top of the house. The Giant who

46

had picked me up on arrival turned out to be one of the grown-up cousins Herbert and our long passage is particularly memorable to me because it was here that he chose to run a model steam engine of which he was the owner. The intricacies of this were far beyond me of course but 'Boy' and I used to be allowed to stand and watch though strictly never to touch. It was a wonderful little model, perfect in every detail and capable of whistling, snorting and spitting steam in the most realistic way. It was very heavy whereas our little trains which ran on rails were light and even to the infantile mind incapable of staying very firmly in the required upright position unless one loaded them so that they only moved at a snail's pace. The model had no rails but ran unerringly in a straight line from one end of the passage to the other. My admiration was unbounded, but being 'only a girl' it was to Boy that all the explanations of details and mechanics were addressed. Boy was allowed occasionally into the 'smoking room' which led off the first flight of stairs below, being on these occasions accepted in theory as 'one of the men', a very special conces-sion of course for it was a strictly private den! We very seldom saw the Cousins, or my Aunt and Uncle during the day, but were brushed up, dressed and sent down to the drawing room for an hour before going to bed, and my aunt usually read to us or we played mildly 'drawingroom games'.

From our vantage point in the nursery we commanded a view of the garden—three sided, with iron railings round and gates here and there, always kept locked. The gardens were impeccably kept and were accessible to each house overlooking them, the owners of the house having a key. We used to see other small neighbours playing there and I vaguely think we did once or twice play with them but were always conscious of stern supervision from above. I have the impression that contact with other children was not smiled upon; and we were usually taken for walks instead. On one occasion I remember enquiring why the ownership of chickens would prevent the corner house little girl playing with me, not having understood the warning that she had had chicken-pox and I was not on any account to go near her.

My recollections of this period over several years are im-possible to sort out, and I only give them in an uncertain order as they come to me. Here are one or two details of the house. There was a semi-basement with area steps and railings; on the front door level on the left as one went in was the dining room, behind it my uncle's study and I think the butler's pantry and domestic offices, but it was an unexplored region and in fact strictly forbidden. Then the smoking room on the first bend of the wide stairs, and my aunt's bedroom, bathroom and dressing room opened off the stairs and also from the drawing room which was L shaped and had a door in the far corner. The next floor consisted of bedrooms, bathrooms etc. and the only part of the house which really concerned us was the top floor, from which we could look down over (or through) the bannisters with a full view of the wide 'cage d'escalier' below. No maid was ever to be seen and the nurseries must have been cleaned while we were out and 'well out of the way'. There were thick carpets, shining stair rods, and everywhere sound, massive furniture. Some family portraits, but nothing at all artistic though well arranged I imagine for that period, and everything bearing out Grandmamma's strict ruling that all curtains and materials should be of excellent quality.

On very blustery days (and there were many) we were taken for our walk to the Dean cemetery near by. It seems a curiously lugubrious idea in reality, on the part of our governess who hated wind, but a then-popular turn of mind perhaps and on a par with the statement in one of her favourite verses (*We are Seven*) that 'she took her little porringer and ate her supper there'. We knew all the paths, the ivy grown walls, and many of the tombstones and often visited that of our little cousin, a little white cross against a distant wall. The cemetery was part of a veritable ravine spanned in another part by the Dean Bridge and its differences of ground level, groups of trees and ivy covered walls made it very sheltered. One forgot the violent winds which came in from the sea and raged everywhere else so that at certain exposed corners people were occasionally literally blown off their feet. One day in the cemetery I came upon a little featherless bird lying on the path. It had fallen from the nest—its little body blue and cold, the skin seemingly barely covering the internal organs from which protruded head and legs—it gave me a sudden shock and made

48

an unforgettable impression. To digress from my own memories to a letter obviously written at this period to India, I find that it recounts that Boy had a new game. He built a sort of box with his bricks and was heard quoting from the Creed 'dead and buried, descended into Hell', wrapping up a brick and popping it into the box—a bright thought then occurred to him. 'Sybil, come and play Hell with me! it's a lovely game.'

On finer days one of our walks was to Queensferry Road, which led out towards the Forth Bridge and was still bordered in those days by fields and hedgerows. We used to collect groundsel for Aunt Eliza's birds as well as bouquets of common little flowers such as coltsfoot, celandines and birdseye which grew on the verge of ploughed land. This occupation had one advantage; it taught me to see and appreciate anything capable of flowering even in cities, on walls and in ditches! Once on our way to the cemetery we saw a coach show-room and store which had been ravaged by fire the night before. In fact literally burnt out, though the floors must have been solid as I quite clearly remember charred remains visible on an upper floor—carriages, of which only skeleton wheels remained, seemingly the only recognizable remnants. We found the continual wind rather fun sometimes, not however on Sundays when I had to wear a hat made by Cark which apart from being absolutely hideous was quite unsuitable for such weather. It matched my coat and was of brightish blue tweed with natural colour ostrich feathers trimming a brim stiffened with buckram, so that once off it would roll happily like a hoop whipped by the wind and many were the chases I had after it. I rather think that I conveniently found it more comfortable off than on and enjoyed the extra exercise. I don't fancy it was the right shape for my head anyway and keeping it on must have been a question of balance. It only had a narrow elastic under the chin and no doubt the wider stiff and crackling satin ribbon ('good quality') substituted on later hats was intended to be an improvement!

Our Aunt Eliza ('Lady P' to everyone else) was I think very insensitive where children were concerned, and probably more used to boys anyway. The only time I saw her was when we were dressed and sent down for an hour before bedtime and usually read a delightful, well-worn and profusely illustrated book about the Pig family. 'Tis Sarah Pig you now behold', and when Sarah employed the warming pan on the back of an agressive Mastif the piglets cried out joyfully 'that's right Ma! give him another smack.' Then there was Little Black Sambo, his beautiful clothes and his pancakes and other tales of the same series. I don't remember my aunt ever coming up to our nursery, and even in the Highlands she only took a comfortable, kindly and rather impersonal interest and never occupied herself actively with us in any way. I have the impression that she never put herself in a child's place or attempted to do so. It is difficult to explain, but there was little or no individual contact with her as with Unk. The nearest she ever got to cuddling us was when seated squarely in an armchair, a hassock under her feet, she took me on her knee to my discomfort and embarassment and pressed me against a well-corseted figure—'keep quiet'—while she read to me.

She ran the household entirely through the medium of governess and domestic and was in effect a figurehead and held, as such, an unassailable position. Her attitude in the case of nephew and niece was understandable, but probably an indication of character, as I was once told that with her own boys she left all management of school and college affairs and interviews in this connection to their father. Also all one summer when her own little daughter was obviously far from well and too weak to move about much, so that her father carried her about though she was a child of twelve or so, she still apparently was unconcerned and did not realize that the child was terribly ill. In fact she was dying of consumption. With all this Aunt Eliza was extremely kind; she had always been rather spoilt and thought a lot of as the eldest of her family, and had never had to rough it, so that she had a comfortable feeling of well-being and of things and people 'as they should be'. She gave out in fact a reassuring sense of stability and spread an atmosphere around her so that one had the feeling that anything which didn't fit in was simply non-existent. She had been the eldest of a large family, and had, at home when she first grew up, never been allowed to go out walking alone but must take her youngest sister in a pram, the idea being that people would take her for a married woman and would not accost her! She had a long engagement as her fiance was not considered financially in a position to marry in spite of a career which promised to be brilliant. But once engaged she was allowed to go out to a Society family in Rome where the two sons, good looking and full of charm, both fell for her. She had a good time, went about a lot, and was also given singing lessons—and I believe was told she had a good enough voice to take it up professionally. 'Incredible suggestion!' Upon this she was brought home and married off safely to her fiance. They were quite well off, entertained a lot and led a social life, both in London and Edinburgh, knowing everyone there was to be known at the time. When we lived there she still gave fairly frequent dinner parties, and used to sing to her guests. She was tall and well made with dark hair bordering on chestnut—'majestic' is the word I would apply to her, as I remember her in those days on the few occasions when I caught a glimpse of her dressed to receive her guests, her magnificent hair piled up and caught with shining star and crescent in diamonds. My uncle had wide-set eyes, clear-cut features and side whiskers, and they were unquestionably an extremely good-looking couple. I think Sir Charles was very widely admired and liked, and we as children both adored him—'Unk' to us. It was his atmosphere in particular which pervaded the house, an atmosphere of justice, kindliness and understanding in spite of his being a very busy man. In all the years we were there I never heard a cross word, an argument or criticism. If there were any it was not within our hearing, which applies also to my own family when we were young. Though it is obvious that this idea must have been comparatively easy to live up to when nursery and schoolroom each had its own very secluded existence with ample staff to cope with all emergencies.

Cark had an unfortunate habit of playing off one child against the other and, looking back, we seldom seem both to have been in her good books at the same time. Boy was the more popular, and I was surprised to notice one day that when he had been sent to bed in disgrace for some seemingly insignificant reason, she occupied herself in the night nursery rigging up a suitable light and taking photos of him in his dressing gown to send to India! I think it was the already obvious masculine element which attracted her! He was a lovely sturdy child—rosy-cheeked and well-made, only really just emerging from babyhood but every inch a boy, which probably accounted for the fact that 'Boy' was about this time largely substituted for 'Michael', though when we were spoken of together it was always 'Sybil and Michael'. I was on the other hand shy and nervous, very feminine, contemplative and earnest, and became very subdued. I never remember at any time quarrelling or fighting or even having words with Michael. We played very happily and amused ourselves together. I was no doubt a difficult child. Cark at any rate found me so, and also found that force—her favourite weapon—got nowhere with me. Boy was of a happy disposition, and being over a year younger excuses were made for him on this score. I never remember resenting this all the same, or feeling in the least jealous; and in most of our adventures at that time we were inseparable. I don't think that it entered into either of our heads that grown-ups could possibly be wrong, so that any resentment we felt was entirely subconscious. It was easy to reduce us to obedient silence, but for my part I recollect being puzzled and upset at the motives attributed to me and her antagonism only raised in me a stubborn barrier, making me feel hard and empty. When she found me particularly unmanageable, she'd say 'you can go down to your uncle' and I would creep downstairs to knock gently on his door—a long way, and each step seemed wide! 'Yes, what is it?' he would say, turning on his swivelled chair from in front of a large desk always piled with papers, its open drawers filled with bundles of them all tied up with pink tape (to my eyes it was pink, though I suppose it was what is usually known as 'red tape'). Speechless, I would go in, adjusting my white pinafore as I went. 'What is the matter? Come and tell me about it'—And he would lift me on to his knee with a smile. In a second, all my bottled up hardness had vanished, and very soon he was in possession of a reluctant story of the sequence of events, plain, unvarnished and strictly truthful as seen from my point of view. I feel pretty sure that he talked things over with my governess and smoothed them out to my advantage though never putting her in the wrong. He never attempted to punish me, and I don't think he ever told me I

52

was wrong or naughty, but he never in any way interfered with Cark's authority. I am inclined to think that it was largely a question of nerves and the weight of responsibility on top of a very strict upbringing—a large family in a country doctor's household. She was extraordinarily strong-willed and imposed her will so that neither Boy nor I would ever have dreamed of criticizing, complaining or even admitting to anyone how hard she was, and though never rebelling outwardly we were I suppose in a curious way fond of her, as children are apt to accept what they recognize as Fate without demur.

Sybil with Sir Charles Pearson, 'Unk', June 12, 1898

Much as I am inclined to blame people who voluntarily take on the job of looking after children when they have no real aptitude for it or love of children as such, I can understand that from the point of view of the parents our governess may have seemed excellent and had been thoroughly recommended. She was scrupulously honest and reliable, and there could in any case be no easy choice for parents gone abroad even though leaving children and governess in a household which in many ways was ideal. Our physical well-being was in general very well attended to I think, but I can remember on one particular occasion being really ill with a cold (the nasty details of which I will not go into) and can feel again the misery and loneliness at night. I would judge now that I had sinus trouble, and it is no exaggeration to say that I went through agonies struggling miserably to keep my sniffling and choking muffled under the bedclothes. I was slapped soundly and told to keep quiet, my cot being unfortunately within reach of the governess, who liked a peaceful night, and could lean over the foot of her bed and administer heavy-handed punishment every time now and then though I was doing my utmost to keep quiet during seemingly endless hours. Our existence was, except for an hour in the evening, entirely a nursery life, and I remember well on occasion peeping over the bannisters to see the guests arriving and mounting the wide stairway to the drawing room; and later, the couples having been sorted out, going down the stairs again to the dining room. Dodds would then take over and supervise with extra domestics bustling in and out with plates and dishes. I can't remember Cark at all on these occasions, and think that having 'put us safely to bed' she must have joined the grown ups. We would scarcely have been watching the show had she been in the nursery, and many letters to India speak of 'the help she was able to give my aunt by making herself useful in all sorts of ways'. My eldest cousin had become engaged and it was a particular joy to us when his fiancee used to rush upstairs to talk to us at odd moments —sometimes dressed for these dinner parties, sometimes during the day, and her face, framed in jet black hair, would light up with a smile when she caught sight of us peeping over the bannisters. She had a trick when she knew I had been in

54

disgrace of saying 'there's that little black monkey sitting on your shoulder again!' and I can remember turning my head in surprise to look for him. Dodds the butler was a great friend of ours; our bathroom at the top of the house and his pantry on the ground floor both opened into the same ventilation chimney, and we'd often hear him whistling and could shout to him from our bathroom. On the red-letter occasions when everyone was out he must presumably have been told to keep an eye on us and there were uproarious games with him downstairs; it must have been in the dining room, as I definitely connect it with leather chairs. There were at least two large leather arm-chairs and a great number of other chairs round the table and against the walls. He used to pile chairs to make a 'carriage and horses'. We'd go for a drive or scramble about amongst the chairs, inventing all kinds of games and laughing as we never did upstairs till we were hot and exhausted. It was always surprising after these marvellous games, jumping, running and climbing over the chairs, to see Dodds quite imperturbable and sphinx-like as ever the next time we met him! He was the Perfect Butler. On the occasions when we went out driving with the carriage and pair he would be dressed like Campbell the coachman in a smart green livery and tall hat with cockade. He then sat arms crossed like an image, and only came to life when it was necessary to leap down and open the carriage door or ring a front door bell. He eyed us at these times with a stony stare and one had to look hard to note an occasional twinkle.

We used to hear regularly from our parents and wrote to them weekly under strict supervision, but the notes were short and copper-plate, often re-written with tears and we never told them any of the things that were so important to us nor probably that they most wanted to hear. There was only an occasional letter said to be written un-aided. About this time came the news that the baby sister Ruth had died in India. We had of course only known her as an infant-in-arms, and though we had seen snap-shots since all this naturally seemed vague and confused with our immediate surroundings and occupations, the transition from baby-photos to the little white cross leaving a gap which was not easily realizable and scarcely understood. I will include here a scene described by

55

Cark writing out to India, though I don't remember it. She wrote: I told Sybil that 'the baby sister had gone to live with God in Heaven'. 'Do you mean Mother won't bring her with her when she comes back?' 'No—but she is so happy singing songs in Heaven.' 'How can she sing when she can't talk?'

Duneaves

Boy and I were very bad travellers, as I have said, always sick, and when Unk didn't come with us he prepared a wonderful parcel 'for the train' with biscuits, fruit, sweets, toys and oddments of all sorts, each carefully wrapped up in tissue paper and tied with his familiar pink tape. He said it would keep us occupied and we'd forget to be sick, and in fact the thrills and excitement over that box more than justified his idea and the imagination and care which those little parcels represented. For the long holidays he would come up too, but I fancy he always followed later, only appearing when the household was established and running smoothly. For the grown-ups it was a time of real relaxation, rest and loosening of the prevailing formality of town—a truly simple life in every way, as I remember it, though of course made easy by an expert staff and in that way very different from anything we or our children knew after the wars which came later and shattered habits and conceptions even in Britain, so that often one woman took on the work of 3 or 4 servants, and life was reduced almost to that of peasants for many of those who for one reason or another gave up trying to keep up the staff and standards of 'before 1914', that far off and curiously different epoch. Some of the maids came up with us, the rest following, and here we made friends with several of them. The only one who lived there more or less permanently, was old Ann, the housekeeper. I believe she went home to her house in the neighbouring town for the winter months. She was fat and comfortable with a smiling face, double chin and intelligent eyes, and she was a real friend of ours. I visited her many years later after she retired and she still had the same infectious laugh and beaming smile. Donald the gardener, a familiar figure to us, was always about. He was untalkative, but kindly and bearded— and was certainly a most efficient gardener. All his tools, including a huge scythe, were kept in a wooden shed under some beech trees near the back drive. I had a horror of this scythe and wouldn't go near the place. A scythe even now gives me a shuddering down the back, and as I can recollect no incident which could have frightened me, I think the fear must have been deliberately instilled by Cark. Another figure we knew well was that of Peter the Gamekeeper who often called on his tour of the valley and hillside. He was a huge man, very good looking, with a long beard and grey-blue eyes under heavy brows and always carried a stick and had a dog with him. Curiously enough, I was talking, more than 20 years later, to a woman in a little Inn by the lake and she seemed at first suspicious of my English accent. But when I noticed a photo of the game-keeper I remembered so well on her wall and exclaimed 'That's Peter!', she thawed at once and realized I was authentic. In fact she put me up and fed me delicious scones and farm butter such as in England I had not tasted.

At Duneaves, there were large semi-basement premises with kitchen etc. where the staff had their rooms. We also saw them every day when before breakfast the whole household met for prayers, and they trooped in to the dining room where a row of chairs was already arranged for them along the wall. Ann and the other maids all wore well fitted and always spotless striped cotton dresses—incidentally, the staff always included a laundry maid, as everything was washed at home. Dodds brought up the rear of the file and closed the door. I remember noticing that old Ann had some difficulty in kneeling when, after my uncle had read a short passage from the huge Family Bible on a table in front of the side window, everyone knelt for a few minutes before they all filed out again. Bowls of porridge were then brought in to be followed usually by eggs just brought up from the farm.

We children profited from the loosening of many of our restrictions, there being only one room at our disposal at Duneaves so that we were much more with the family, which at this time included one or more of the three sons and their fiancees who all packed into the house somehow: no one dressed even in the evenings. It seems to me, looking back, that it was always summer! I wore cotton frocks and Boy jersey and knickers and we were out all day. 'The glory and the dream' indeed for us! and comparable in its special way to no other period of my life. What a respite it must have been for Unk and 'the boys'. The house though comfortable was almost primitive in the simplicity of its furnishings—a few solid useful tables and chairs, but otherwise wicker arm chairs and well worn curtains of coloured serge, and table cloths the same and in some rooms muslin curtains. In the centre of the drawing room stood a huge bird-cage with gold-finches, green-finches and siskins who were often transferred to smaller cages and put out in the garden, some of them even flying into the trees and returning. And Coco the Squirrel who also amused himself in the trees of the garden and came home when he felt inclined—but the first year he was a baby out of the nest, and lived in a box lined with soft hay and red flannel, lapping milk out of a spoon, and never going further afield than the drawing room. He was the sweetest little creature—bright brown with tufts on his ears and a cream coloured tail and vest, as they usually had up there where they were numerous, though there were no grey ones. Coco was as tame as possible and when he came to a nut would look at us, his brilliant eyes sparkling and watchful as he sat on his hind legs to enjoy it, holding it tightly in his neat little paws. He was mischievous too as he used to stand on his hind legs and pull at any flowers in vases until with a crash he brought the whole thing down on top of him. Then he would scuttle off up a curtain with a nut and sit looking good as gold.

The house stood in the Glen above a bend of the wide river with its crystal-clear water and pebbles or sand beaches. The only means of getting to the nearest village church was to row over and then walk a mile or so, and a flat-bottomed boat was kept for that purpose and moored near the farm where there was a deepish passage. If the boat was on the wrong side one had to shout for it, but it was considered a serious means of transport and of course not to be used by children alone. On one side of the river there was only the farm, woods—fields—the unique road, though passage for horse traffic, being not much more than a track leading from field to field and wood, and whether one chose to turn right or left there were, either way, five or six gates which had to be opened and shut before arriving at a bridge by which to cross to the better road on the far side of the river, which led either up the Glen or to the railway junction a good many miles away. Campbell was always at hand with a pair of horses and the wagonette, and lodged above the stables down by the river. Campbell was I believe, entirely responsible for the pair of horses he brought up, which must have been hired and were not the ones he used in town—and one of the stipulations was that they must be entirely reliable and used to the occasional cars one might meet. Many horses still were not used to these noisy monsters, now becoming more frequent, and would not pass them and of course on steep and rough roads with many turnings and steep falls or rock on either side, this could be very dangerous. The wagonette was the only vehicle in use, and the great treat was to be allowed to sit beside Campbell on the box.

What endless hours we spent paddling by that river!—fishing sometimes with crooked pins which fortunately rarely enticed the fish though I remember once permitting a fish I'd caught (the size of a sardine) to be cooked for my supper. In summer the banks of luscious grass waist high were full of wild-roses, lupins, oxeye daisies, cornflowers and all sorts of flowers growing in the long grass. There was an island down-stream from which we usually played, which was blue with lupins and fringed with small whitish pebbles. A swiftly-flowing current swept in at the far side of the river where the main stream had hollowed a bed but on our side the river was perfectly safe and generally speaking shallow. Further up the Glen there were deep pools overhung by rocks and quite good fishing to be had—smallish brown trout, as in the other burns rushing down from the hills. There is something unforgetable about these Scottish rivers and burns with their clarity as one looks down into the still pools or quick moving water flowing over peat or over shining golden-brown pebbles and gravel, sometimes shallow and trickling gently, sparkling in the sunlight; at other times rushing swollen and forceful as rain collects and sweeps down from every tiniest hollowed crevice in the heath-covered moors above.

About half way up our hill was the deer fence which kept them at a distance, though we often saw them when, sitting beside Campbell, we learned to use our eyes. He unbent completely when out of town and had marvellous eyes for such things. He always spotted the deer long before any of us noticed them as also the mushrooms growing in the fields stretching down to the loch. To get to this loch which was a favourite object for a drive, we left our glen by a track which followed a break in the hills on our side of the river. On reaching the summit one could suddenly see the loch, a vast expanse stretching below us, and we could then follow the road for miles above with a splendid view of the water. There were of course other expeditions and sometimes we would leave Campbell on the road while we climbed up beside a stream to picnic high on the hills, Meganwy, Glen Golendy & Scheilallion, and even to a further valley as far as Tunnel Bridge, one of the loveliest of the little old bridges spanning a perfect torrent of foam alternating with rocks and deep pools. These expeditions were for us in the early days only occasional and for the most part the river, garden, hillside and wood supplied all our wants; when we went in the wagonette for a day's outing it was quite usual for us to fall asleep in the arms of a grown-up on the return journey, happily worn out with the excitement and the sunshine—I was often wakened early on a summer morning by the sound of Donald raking the wide stretch of gravel outside our windows, and even now more than sixty years later, when I hear the sound of a rake I am transported in a twinkling to that enchanted spot. There were huge beech trees where the drive curved and led down past a spring (which had been walled in round the back and served as a fridge almost lost among ferns) to the stables and the river. In front of the house was a lawn; long grass beyond it where the short drive led between plane trees to a gate opening into the farm lane running on the one hand straight to the farm and on the other to the rough and only road on our side of the river. Beyond the lawn was a thick hedge and wicket gate enclosing a large square flower and vegetable garden. Not far beyond that rose the hill, topped with pines and heather. There were numberless rabbits and the hedge was reinforced with wire netting. So that on the very few

60

occasions when a particularly persistent rabbit got in he must have felt rather like Peter Rabbit squeezing under the gate into Mr McGregor's garden, and he wouldn't for long escape the vigilant eye of Donald. A rabbit even on the big lawn in front of the house and in full view of our windows was quite an event and I must admit much appreciated by us, but as a rule the little cotton-tails kept tactfully to the long grass, the fields, hillside and river bank.

The magic of those early morning sights and sounds! Dew on the grass—the vibrating silence, the gradual crescendo of bird-song then the heat of midday and of all nature heavy with blossom and fruit. Showers and sun, so that luscious and plentiful life of all kinds flourished & prepared for the glowing colour of the autumn valley & hills—of the birch, the beech, the rowan and the heather. Inside the wicket gate & hedge was an enchanted garden. Well kept grass paths like green velvet between all the borders, and every flower you can think of growing luxuriantly in masses and still leaving space for roses & thick hedges of sweet peas with stems and blossoms as fine as any I have seen since. Whiffs of sweet briar from the hedge pervaded the air as one's feet moved softly along the grass paths. There was an old gnarled pear tree, cherry trees, apple trees and still room for rows of vegetables of all sorts, strawberries, raspberries and gooseberries. There were occasionally birds, thrushes and blackbird mostly, to disentangle from the fruit nets, & we were given almost daily soup plates piled with strawberries & thick cream. Often we would go out armed with cups of sugar and eat strawberries in the sunshine—or gooseberries when we felt like braving the prickles. Cark, in our private nursery life, maintained that cream or fruit, except in small quantities, made us ill. But here we ate all we wanted and I never remember any bad results. There were masses of crab apples, blackberries, rowans & other berries so the birds had a good supply outside the nets & contented themselves with the addition of succulent worms which were plentiful. From the drive gate beyond the plane trees a magnificent beech avenue led to the wood, passing the farm on its way. A tree was missing here & there, & they must have all been very old, probably dating from the early days of the farm long before the house was built. Once Michael and I found a baby owl sitting blinking at us on the root of one of the beech trees, having fallen out of its nest. The parents used to come & feed it and we supplemented occasionally with tit bits. One of our great treats was to be allowed by 'Jimmy' who had charge of the two sturdy farm horses to ride on the plough, which turned over the ground at great speed leaving in its wake movement enough to interest all the birds in the neighbourhood and the gulls which collected as if by magic when there was a rumour of ploughing in the air. At other

Sybil and Michael with Jimmy and the farm horses at Duneaves, 1898

times there would be the hay and corn cutting machines to watch (they were not safe for us to ride on) and the raking and tossing of the hay. A favourite expedition was to the far end of the beech avenue with a picnic tea, cutting across the river and following it past three fields and across two tiny clear burns till we came to the oak wood. Primroses grew in profusion in spring, & I remember having put bunches of these primroses into the water of the burn to keep fresh while we were having tea, then later finding them with their stems covered apparently by masses of brown stones—in reality tiny insects (cadis worms?) disguised under minute pebbles with which they tried doubtless to make themselves invisible to birds and humans alike. There was a crab apple

62

                                                                    Duneaves
                                                                Aug. 21st.1901

My dear Mother,
    Uncle Charlie is staying hear now. Boy and I got a lot
of wood pigeon's feathers yesterday in the Avenue. It is
going to be a very nice hot day to day. My mignonette
will flower soon I think. Uncle Charlie gave me a Band
of Mercy. Boy gave me a bit of heather that he got in
the Avenue. I think that Boy's flowers will flower soon.
We have been playing in the cornfield and helped to
bind the shevs. With lots of love and kisses
                                                                    Sybil.

tree overhanging the path by the river, & at the right season
we always gathered baskets of the tiny bright fruit, taking it
home to be made into crab apple jelly which was one of Aunt
Eliza's specialities, though whether actually made by her or
the cook I am not quite certain. She superintended anyway
& we were called in to taste and sometimes to stir. All her
jams and jellies looked specially attractive in charming little
coloured bowls & pots, a paper dipped in brandy was laid
directly on top of the jelly & the whole closed with a paper
brushed with white of egg & always carefully labelled &
marked with the date. The whole performance impressed me
enormously & we were always given the skimmings from the
jam for our tea.
    We were quite cut off from the outside world, although I
remember that there were wooden boxes here and there
by the roadside into which letters and packages could be
dropped, to be fetched by faraway farms and cottages on
the hill; our own post arrived in the same way & had to be
fetched by one of the men from the roadside on the far bank
of the river.
    The regime of punishments though relaxed still came into
force occasionally and once Boy had been sent up to his
room on a hot & sunny afternoon for some minor misde-
meanour, & feeling more enterprising than usual was looking
around for something to do. Cark kept her shoes & boots
including Wellingtons in rows under a table by the window.

Sybil and Michael at Duneaves, on the way to the post-box, 1902

A moment's thought & his mind was made up. He started filling all the shoes with water from the jug on the washstand & not having enough he looked again to make sure that the coast was clear, then fetched more water from the bathroom till they were all filled—shoes, Wellingtons, galoshes, everything he could find even down to bedroom slippers. That job satisfactorily concluded, he waited till he was called down to tea. I don't know, but think the escapade amused the family so much (when this was recounted by the scandalized victim) that no reprisals could be taken.

Looking down from that same window one day, having been sent up to lie down, I caught my breath in surprise. On the long grass at the side of the house was our familiar Tartan rug, but what did I see in the middle of it? A huge

64

Birthday cake—candles, sugar icing, twirls & scrolls complete.
And all round it was a mass of pink roses! the sun shone—the
bees buzzed—not a breath stirred the trees. I was five years
old.

Sybil at Duneaves, 1898

*   *   *   *

Minehead
June 4th

My dear Dora
I wish
that I could
go to the
coronation
do not you

it would be _very_
nice I am shure. We
are not going to the
farm till after the
coronation. We can
not feed our silk-
worms on mulberry
liers because there are
not eny mulbery liers
at the farm. The woman

ry went away the
other day we loked
out of a hotel window
and saw the horses
go into the train one
horse ran away but
they caught him one
picked dredfully when
he was in once tum-
bled down in the

train when he got
up his hed was turned
round the rong way
so they had to put it
right He made a ridg
on the sands the other
day. Lots of love
and kisses xxxxxxx
Your loving
Sybil

Sybil to her half-sister Dora, 1902

Bijbehara,
June 28th.1902.

My darling little Sybil—

Many *many* happy returns of your Birthday. I hope you & Boy & Cark will have a very happy day. How much I wish that I could come and spend it with you at Harewood—but I shall be thinking of you all day. God bless thee, my little precious Sybil.

Fancy being eight years old—such a *big* girl! I hope you are being *very* good, because as we grow older we aught to grow better every day that we live.

Father and Dora and I have sent you a little parcel, and we hope it will arrive safe and that you will like what is in it. I wonder if you will have got it when this letter arrives.

We are still in the place with the funny long name—Bijbehara—we have our tents up and I daresay we shall stay for several days, until the weather gets quite settled. We have had a good deal of rain but this is a lovely day. Father has not been quite well, but he is better today, I am glad to say.

Thank you very much indeed for your nice letter. What *beautiful* paper Aunt Eliza sent you! Monica was very much delighted with her 'Coronation Book'—she laughed when I gave it to her and began to turn over all the pages and look at the pictures. You said she was to wear it, so I fastened it onto her with a pin and she wore it all day. You see its *just* arrived in time, didn't it?

You must write and tell me *all* about your Birthday, and what you did all day, but I daresay you won't have time just at once, because you may perhaps have other letters to write.

Now I am going to tell you a story!

STORY

I am a baby crow, and I live at a place in Kashmir called Bijbehara. I am rather nice looking, at least so I heard my mother say one day when she was talking to a brown hoopoe who had got a baby at the same time. I think the hoopoe fancied her baby was handsomer but my mother told my father she never heard such nonsense so of course the hoopoe

67

must have been mistaken. I am black with a fluffy, dark grey breast, and I have pale blue eyes with bright red spots in the middle of them.

I have two brothers, and we were all quite happy in our nest, until one day our mother said it was quite time for us to learn to fly, as we had plenty of feathers, and then a *dreadful* thing happened to me. I was just sitting on the edge of the nest, and my mother was telling me how to spread out my wings, but I was afraid to start, and my father got rather impatient, and gave me a poke, and I lost my balance and fell off the branch, and went down, down, down, down, until I landed with a terrible flop on the green grass beneath our beautiful chenar tree. For a moment I felt quite silly, then I sat up and began to look about me.

There were several curious two-legged things sitting under the chenar—they had come from the river two days before, and my mother had said they were 'sahibs', and would not do any harm to crows—they were all sizes, one *very* big, and one very little. The little one was called Mona, and it came to look at me—and it shouted, and laughed, & danced round me, and its ayah took me up and gave me to it to hold—and oh! I *was* so frightened—and oh! it did hold me *so* tight—and its hands were small, and fat, and very strong—and one of the middle-sized sahibs (who had no legs at all, only two feet) said 'Gently, Baby—you are squeezing the poor little crow too tight'—and then they put me down on the grass again—and the ayah made me sit on a stick, and the middle-sized sahib said, 'Oh! how neat Baby looks with the crow', and she ran and got a black box, and made something go 'click' in it, and then all the sahibs laughed—and my mother (who was sitting up in the trees all the time calling out 'ao' 'ao', which meant 'come back') said 'See, child, how handsome you are—they have made a picture of you'—but I don't know what my mother meant atall.

Anyway the 'Mona' sahib played with me all the afternoon on the grass, and though I was very frightened at first, I got quite accustomed to her, and did not mind her fat hands so much.

I spent all night on the ground, and it was *very* cold, and I wished I were back in my warm nest—and I thought it rather

68

unkind of my mother not to come down and sit on top of me, but she said she could not leave my brothers.

This morning the 'Mona' sahib played with me again, but while she was having her breakfast the very big sahib came and took hold of me with both hands and threw me with all his might up into the tree—I went up, up, up—I thought I should be killed, but at last I came fluttering down upon a big branch, and managed to catch hold of a little twig firmly with both my claws, and so here I am in the end sitting up in my beautiful chenar tree again, and I shall take good care not to tumble out of it any more.

I like 'Mona' sahib best when I can see her at a distance.

But my mother says, 'See what a handsome crow our son is! Did you ever hear of any other crow having his photograph taken?'

It seems to me my mother is getting a little silly in her old age.

THE END

*   *   *   *

Minehed.

~~Jan~~ Feb. 7th

My dear Mother.

Thank you very mutch for the post card with the picture of an Indian grocer it <u>is</u> a funny one I will make you a picture of the one here. I am culecting post cards now Francie sent me several of places in Jersy. We took a cab to Steert lane, below Harwood yesterday to get some Snowdrops they grow quite wild in <u>such</u> quantities there. They are <u>so</u> pritty, we got 7 bunches and then we did not get anything like all, they were perfectly lovely I wish you could see them is it not a pitty they will be over by the time you are home I am ~~sho~~ sure you would like to see them. I am writing a long letter this week to ocupy your time going home from Southhampton to London. We went to Dunster for a walk the other day and on the way we found a white Violet. An other day we went right round by the golf links and round by Dunster and home again, it was about the longgest walk we have had. Mrs Clark has looked after us several times lately while Cark and Miss Wiggie have gone out bicycling. It was such a nice fine sunny day yesterday. I got another post card today from Francie, I have got 10 now counting the one you sent me. It seems quite funny to think of us all being together again. The Snowdrops in my pot are coming out beautifully. The birds are so funny, we can hardly get Rex into his eggs, he is so knowing, he hops out when Cark gets up to shut him in, and he knows quite well what we meen when we ask him if he wants a hemp, they both like Bananas or a bit of Orange or Apal or grape or any sort of green food. Cark is making Lady Rose a dark blue serge coat, Lady Rose is one of my dolls I have got 13 dolls counting all the tiny ones but 4 are teny weny ones how many has Mona got now. I hope you are having a nice voyage and that the sea is not too rough. We picked some palm the other day out for our ~~room~~ walk it is so pritty there was lots of it but we could not get mutch because we were on a path and it was growing on a slope. I wish you were here now, I want to see you all so much I really hardly remember Father. We are going to tea at Miss King's on Monday. Lady Rose's coat is finished now I did not know Cark had nearly finished it but I found Lady Rose sitting with it on the nexed day it fits very nicely she looks so nice in it. I washed my dolls clothes yesterday Lady Rose's cap and frock look so nice, and fresh, and clean, they are made of pink muslin with a patern on it, Lady Rose is my bigest doll, not quite as big as Donald Frazer. Our calender of days is getting so tiny it is so nice to see it going, going, going, it is at 5 now? I am so glad you are landing so soon I shall hug you all so much that I shall squese you all to nothing. We went to tea with Mrs Hase yesterday we had great fun Violet Hase has got such a lovely big rocking horse it was quite as big as a donkey, ~~We~~ there were some crackers at tea and there was a dolls muff in one, a little figer in an other, and a book of shadow picturs.

Miss King drove us there and back. Goodbye, I am writing to Father. So lots of love and kisses to you all.

Your loving daughter
Sybil

*   *   *   *

George and Dora, back in England

Sybil, on the same occasion

Home from India and Lincombe

When my parents finally came home from India I was eight and I think very young for my age. There had of course been other visits, but this was the first time for years that we were together as a family, and for us there was the added excitement of seeing the little sister who had been born in Edinburgh, and gone out to India as an infant. She was now three and went by the name of Bunda—a misspelling of Hindustani as it stood for Monkey and only connected in my mind years later with Kipling's Banda-log (monkey-people) in the *Jungle Book*. She used a good many words of Hindustani, having picked them up from her Ayah & other native servants, and was a fascinating little creature, chubby and fair haired, always attracting attention and admiration when we went out. I have no recollection curiously enough of meeting my parents after such a long parting—although I clearly remember anticipating it. It all seems to have been obliterated by an overwhelming bustle and movement in strange surroundings in London. We didn't see much of my parents at this time. They were very occupied and I suppose being in rather cramped lodgings with no garden our movements were strictly organized! But we always went down to the drawing room after tea and played games or amused ourselves with picture books but my principal recollection is of stories being read to Bunda—She demanded attention and though only three she knew every favourite by heart and would correct anyone who dared to skip or alter even a word. They were well-worn books with large coloured old-fashioned illustrations and seemed vaguely familiar to me which I suppose is quite possible. Sometimes Mother called me into her room when she was dressing, & I considered it a great privilege to be allowed to 'do up her dress' for her, a performance entailing the manipulation of endless hooks & eyes down the back which was tackled on my part with conscience and loving care.

We spent some months in very drab lodgings in London before finding a country house. There was a smell of dust, plush, and anti-macassars, and the house seemed to me inordinately

74

dark. It was a dismal place as I remember it, in a small street near Paddington Station, the landlady buxom and kindly with a golden wig and ample bosom and I always thought (though what gave me this impression I don't know) an eye for the main chance. We were taken to the Zoo, Madame Tussaud's, and the Tower, but the usual daily routine was to Hyde Park with the pram. We always set off for the Park armed with a paper bag & Bunda invariably ate a quantity of the crusts intended for the birds & ducks on the Serpentine long before we got there. On special occasions we went to Whiteley's Pet Department where there were at that time Jereboas and a variety of doormice, guinea pigs, puppies and other animals.

Once Princess Mary and the Prince of Wales arrived at Paddington by train, and by mere chance we happened to pass with the nurse and pram along the road parallel to the station entrance, the latter on a lower level as it still is. We had front seats so to speak, clutching the bars of the railings which separated the road from the station entrance below, and gazing down at the Princess and the small crowd collected on the platform.

My first theatre dates from this time. We were taken by my father, and it was a breath-taking adventure with Red Indians and a waterfall on what seemed a very vast stage. I think it must have been a Drury Lane performance. Men and Women in a canoe shot the rapids into a lake of real water pursued by Red Indians to whom the waterfall surprisingly proved an effective barrier! I was glued to my seat with horror and anticipation, but suppose that all ended well as I remember nothing more, though that scene is indelible!

We went through a nightmare summer with measles each in turn, supposedly caught from the monkeys at the Zoo, and followed up with whooping cough, and a consequent scuttling of crowds around us for weeks afterwards whenever we went to the Park as, though not infectious, the whooping cough was obvious.

After London we settled in an old-fashioned looking creeper-clad house in the Midlands, 'Lincombe', which for some reason seemed dismal to me in spite of some happy memories. It was admittedly a banal house but I think the impression was largely due to the shrubberies of fir, yew and laurels which I've always hated since that time, and connect with a strong smell of musty dead leaves and sticks in hidden sunless patches. There was no view in any direction, but an open lawn in front of the house with a field and high hedges beyond. A monkey-puzzle stood on a higher lawn to the right (looking from the house) & was reached by a flight of a few stone steps. Still further to the right was the kitchen garden & orchard and on the drive side of the house was a smaller lawn dotted with ornamental shrubs & very set flower beds.

Church on Sundays was always quite an event. First we got dressed, and this was a martyrdom as the Sunday clothes which had hounded me from early days were always uncomfortable —possibly they were my governess's idea of the equivalent of a hair shirt? The elastic which kept my weekday hat from flying away was at this period replaced on my Sunday hat by rather wide good-quality satin ribbon which was tied in a bow under my chin, and which scraped and crackled as if I was walking on particularly noisy dry leaves. I couldn't move my head with comfort, and had to stay still as a mouse if I wanted to hear anything but I would never have dared complain, any more than in a boot shop, once having said that new shoes were comfortable, I would have admitted that they hurt me when I walked. For such complaints or mistakes my governess was without understanding and as she ruled the schoolroom with a rod of iron after all the years my parents had been in India, I should never have dared to do anything without her approval or to go to my mother when in trouble. This I am sure looking back on it entailed a great deal of unhappiness for my mother who was with us for the first time in years and was not strong-minded enough (nor probably had she the health) to fight the situation. So Sunday started off badly.

The church was some way off and we had to drive there. The horse preferred being ridden, & was always unwilling to go between the shafts. He was a big beast not used to the dog-cart which my father always drove at the time I am thinking of. We children had to be ready in the hall; hair brushed, Sunday clothes & gloves on, and as soon as the groom came round with the dog-cart there would be a silent but determined scramble to climb into the back seat, for the horse had ideas of his own and had no intention of waiting for anyone. He would deliberately do his utmost to back violently into the drawing room window with the groom hanging desperately at his head, for he was a very small man, the horse large and the dog-cart high. Once up we clung firmly to our tilting seat and waited for the rest of the party to climb up in front or join us on the back seat; then my father would quickly gain his seat & seize the reins for to avoid disaster there was not a moment to be lost, and we would set off with a jolt, and a great crunching of gravel. From there it was fairly plain sailing, but one had to walk up any steep hill and this was a ticklish job too for if 'the Brown' was asked to stop on a hill he would again try to back. The best plan was to stop the dog-cart diagonally across the road (there was seldom any traffic) then one might slide rapidly to the ground before the horse realized what was happening and so one found oneself safely on the road without attracting his attention! Finally one would arrive at the church possibly looking rather dishevelled but still clutching prayer-books & feeling immensely relieved. All this was hardly conducive as may be imagined to a tranquil or reverent frame of mind. However we collected hassocks and prayer books (for anyone who had not brought his own) and prepared to make the best of a necessarily agitating morning. I frequently felt sick in the middle of the service and had to go and sit in the porch, which made a pleasant interlude, and when the last hymn had been sung there was an exodus to the church-yard where everyone collected in groups & there was a great deal of polite conversation; any new hat or frock was duly noted to be commented upon later, and after what seemed an eternity we again set off. On the return journey there was no trouble as I suppose 'the Brown' was pleased with the turn events were taking, & was thinking of the bran & oats waiting for him at home.

When Bunda reached church-going age she managed things much better than I. On Sunday mornings regularly towards ten o'clock she began to droop and look pale. She had a very fetching way of blinking down-cast eyes as she murmured 'I don't fink I feel speshly well today' and, reality or imagination, she got away with it!

I have got to admit that generally speaking I looked on going to church on Sundays as rather a farce. Perhaps I exaggerate for I was not in the least irreligious. I was taken as a matter of course but over the years I was struck by the apparent lack of simplicity and as I grew older by the almost invariable insincerity of the whole performance. It was accepted as 'the thing to do', and beyond that didn't mean much to me nor did it appear to be taken very seriously by the rest of the congregation. In fact, preciously as one respected and believed in Christ's teaching, it appeared to have little or no connection with what men made of it. The occasional joyous atmosphere of a carol service, the peace of even-song or the thrill of hearing a good sermon made things come alive and gave me something to think about, but were exceptions, and I always found prayer & contact with things Divine more easily amongst trees, clouds and open spaces—or even in an empty church. A wrong approach to church-going no doubt, but perhaps not a bad one to the truths of all religion. My feeling is that one should never insist on taking a child to church unless he wants to go & this is confirmed for me by my daughter's experience at school. I told her she could go to any service if she wished—Catholic, Protestant or other. She was taken to a Protestant church and was horrified by a tirade from the pulpit against Catholicism which she vehemently described to me as being in the most rabid and un-Christian spirit.

For us there was the occasional red-letter Sunday when my father took us for a walk in the afternoon; usually to the river, and this entailed crossing the orchard and some fields and taking a steep path down through the woods. On our way we usually found and removed wires set by poachers, and then cut across a field where I remember autumn crocuses, to the river. There was a lock here which was a great source of interest to us. Occasionally Father hired a boat for an hour or so, and it was then that I learned to row, not always without tears as each of us had an oar and Michael being younger I had to go on the seat behind him and was told to keep pace with his somewhat erratic strokes. I was not very clever at this which exasperated my Father who had a quick temper and probably didn't much appreciate our rowing capacities. The storm soon cleared but these scenes though mild were my first conscious experience of the masculine temperament!

He had been stationed for so many years in India that we scarcely knew him, so these walks remain vivid as one of the few chances I had of being with him.

I remember that he had not much use for the practice of Christianity generally current in India during his service there. As he described it, the natives were told on Sundays that 'all Men were Brothers' and were kicked around for the rest of the week. Admittedly a converted Christian was seldom the best type, as is suggested by the following factual incident which my Father used to recount with a dry humour; a Padre he knew in India required a new Bearer or House Boy and put up a notice to this effect at the entrance to his compound. Underneath the notice he wrote clearly and firmly 'no Christian need apply'.

From now on I had a fairly strict schoolroom programme and schoolroom and nursery gradually separated themselves. There were only occasional escapes from the still seemingly all-powerful governess who you remember had been with us since I was two. There were one or two special corners in the garden where we hid and played. An arbour of hazel bushes at the end of a rose border, a group of fir trees at the end of the kitchen garden where we each had a patch of our own to cultivate, well hidden behind a thick laurel hedge which ran the length of the kitchen garden between it and the lawn with the monkey-puzzle. Cark was probably just as glad to see us disappear as we were to escape. There were hide-outs too under the musty-smelling firs and laurels which bordered the drive and where we instituted an animal cemetery, burying with great care any dead birds or animals which came to our notice.

There was a farm lane which led into fields at the back of the house; a yard beyond the back door and kitchen opened onto this lane, where were the stables and a huge barn. We often played in this barn (whether with or without permission I don't know!), climbing up ladders to the top of the staked hay and sliding down a precipitous drop from roof level onto the piles of hay on the ground. I don't think Bunda was included in these particular escapades, being too young, but we initiated her into the hazards of negotiating a bridge of branches and twigs over a small and shallow pond in the orchard, and hoped (when she fell in more than once) that the nurse didn't notice her wet socks. Perhaps it says something for the latter's kindliness and sense of humour under an austere exterior that nothing was ever mentioned. For Bunda always wore sandals (from Daniel Neal & Sons) and as she grew was supplied with succeeding sizes of lovely little white socks with a very pretty openwork pattern knitted by Mother. These socks and sandals must often have arrived back in the nursery sopping and far from clean after escapades with us which were very different from the well-conducted walks undertaken with the nurse.

We had several rabbits, Snowball, Smut & Patch & their periodical offspring, but I regret to say that the latter were frequently eaten by their parents; there were dogs & cats too but at that period the dogs were rather impersonal to us children except for a brown-and-white spaniel, Bet—who came for walks & was used for rough shooting, but I don't think any of the dogs lived in the house. We had a donkey too: quite the most stubborn of its kind that I have met, and nothing but a tin can of stones rattled in his ears would move him. Once and only once we induced the nurse to mount this animal, assuring her that he never moved except at a sedate walk, and he (realizing that this was a special occasion) took to his heels and trotted off down the lane to our joy and to the horror of the nurse who however, hung on manfully till the donkey stopped as suddenly as he had started and she landed abruptly but none the worse on terra firma—'Never again!' said she.

There were two huge horses, 'the Black' and 'the Brown', a sturdy cob 'the Brown Pony' and one day a very beautiful slim-legged and dapple-grey pony put in her appearance. She was called Peggy and was for me. But I think it is rather a curious fact that I was never encouraged to think of this as the red letter day it really was for me. It was taken very much as a matter of course and no one seemed to be interested in my immediate reactions, though it would seem to me natural, particularly with a timid child, to encourage her on such an occasion to appreciate and understand and above all express her feelings. For any one of us for that matter to show enthusiasm or even pleasure would have been unusual, but looking back I did in my own quiet way enjoy things all the same. I daresay some of the grown-ups may have been

Sybil on Peggy, The Halesend

sufficiently interested to notice sparkling eyes and suppressed pleasure, but emotion was certainly not encouraged—I had too often in the past been repressed when I rushed forward to throw my arms round my governess for sympathy or understanding. This is not my imagination and must have been obvious as I was told years later by a cousin that she had been very upset to see this repression which led to inability to express spontaneous feelings. It had the far-reaching effect of making a naturally timid child afraid for life of any show of feeling, and God knows the British need encouragement to express their feelings rather than to suppress them!

My father took me out riding fairly regularly, and I suppose that what riding instruction I ever had was given me at that time, but actually it consisted I think mainly in being told to 'sit straight' & one or two obvious comments, for though I had never been on anything more serious than a donkey, I was literally put on a pony and expected to ride—I think it came to me naturally, but there was never any question in those days of a riding school or any special knowledge of how to handle a horse or any of the subtleties taught later

81

generations of young riders. Ignorance, in fact, was bliss, and one just rode to enjoy it (possibly the best way). It was a question of finding 'how to stick on' and instinctively getting to understand one's mount with any fads & fancies he might have. Most of the ponies or horses we had were broken in to some extent of course, but not trained to subtleties in the way which became more or less general later. They were rough to start with and some came from the plough in Ireland. Peggy however had in all probability been passed as a safe child's pony and apart from liveliness she was very manageable & certainly had no vices. Father had ridden all his life beginning with the ponies in the West of Ireland. He was a wonderful horseman and had I think no fear at all of any horse and therefore no inkling that it doesn't come so easily to all children unless they start extremely young. I had no nerves about most adventures and loved animals, but was well scared more than once by his brusque handling of the horses. He always rode 'the Black'—a huge beast with a roman nose who bore a large triangular scar on his flank, the mark of a day's hunting with a previous owner when in jumping a fence a stake had pierced his side, tearing a gaping wound. The horse had gone on as if nothing had happened, his rider, so it was said, being none the wiser until he got home.

The horses used to have a generous supply of oats and were alive to anything which stirred in the hedges or unusual objects they saw in the road. One day we came upon a sack of potatoes left on the wide road. Here was something 'the Black' thought worth making a fuss about, and he did! So much so that my father dismounted and disregarding me and my pony entirely, he led 'the Black' up to the object using his riding crop and kicking the sack till it rattled. 'The Black', his shoes clattering on the surface of the road, snorted, backed and dragged until the reins had slipped over his head and Father was holding them with the horse at the far end. Gradually, however, 'the Black' became interested and approached the sack to investigate. Peggy meanwhile was also interested and was scattering around a short distance away wondering what was going to happen. So did I! but I don't think my father noticed my agitation and having said aloud to 'the Black' 'There! Now you'll know what a sack of potatoes is next time you meet one,' he re-mounted and we went on our way. He turned to me—'The best way of treating a horse one wants to make sure he doesn't do it again—what?' with a half-laugh. This was a trick of his which I remember well—using 'what' broken with a laugh at the end of the sentence in a way which seemed to suggest 'don't you think so?'. Another familiar gesture of his was to turn in the saddle and carry on a conversation, leaning on his hand which he spread palm downwards on the haunch of his mount. These little tricks were to me looking back typical of my father and I have seen my daughter make exactly the same gesture.

I wore for riding a little velvet jockey-cap and a Norfolk jacket with a skirt such as all side-saddle riders wore shaped to fit over the pummels and with breeches underneath. Mother was a good rider and rode occasionally with me on 'the Brown', but I have the impression she didn't care much for riding in England and we seldom went out together. I suppose she was much occupied with housekeeping and nursery affairs, & though I enjoyed rides with her they hadn't the unexpected and exciting element that they had with Father! Michael was far more nervous than I was & had been frightened by a stupid groom who having been told to take him on a leading rein into the paddock for riding practice stood carelessly and made the pony circle round without first making sure the place was free of rabbit holes. Peggy put her foot in one and came down, throwing him but fortunately with no further damage than frightening the boy, but still it was a bad beginning for him.

When my father took us both out I had to ride the brown cob (a good deal larger than my pony) and Boy rode Peggy. A leading rein was always taken & was often thrown to me with the admonition to 'look after the boy'. We sometimes had to pass such alarming things (both for children and ponies) as steam-rollers, and adventures were frequent. One day in winter my mount suddenly slid badly on a patch of ice and came down on her side with me underneath but I was more frightened than hurt. The pony however got loose and set off for home. Peggy thought it would be fun to follow suit; Michael promptly fell off for no real reason, and away went both ponies. My father, having made sure that neither of us was hurt, set off down the road after them on 'the Black'. Away went Gilpin and away. . . . The ponies arrived home first to the consternation of the household and Father eventually came back with them in disgrace. When I had mounted he threw the leading rein to me and told me to look after Peggy—possibly the best way to deal with the rather trembling state of mind and legs.

On these riding expeditions the fear as we approached home was of my reception in the schoolroom on my return, as my father took no count of the time on these occasions and we were often an hour or so later than we expected. Coming in glowing with happiness after a lovely ride with him one day—we had explored a new road and were over an hour late for lunch—my ardour was promptly damped by the reception Cark gave me having worked herself into a state of nerves which vented itself unmercifully on me—this of course well out of earshot of the Parents, behind baize doors.

There were many tears in the schoolroom especially over mathematics at which I have never excelled, and now I realize that the governess was not fitted for teaching and had had probably little or no good ground-work herself. I remember once I had been left alone in the schoolroom. It faced north so there was no sun and only a yard and walls by way of view so that its high north-facing window and a second window in a corner to the West but close to a wall and with dark shrubberies outside, it was not a cheerful room, in fact I remember it as dismal. I was struggling with problems probably primitive but quite beyond me when my sister Dora came in and found me in floods of tears. It was a lovely day and Cark had gone out, but I had been forbidden to leave the room until the sums were finished. My sister sat down and worked with me (though she declared she 'didn't understand the things herself') until we finally got them straight and I was able to disappear into the garden.

There was a change for me when the daughter of one of my father's brother-officers came to stay for a time and did lessons with me. She was the youngest of her family and about my age—a fat cheerful irrepressible child with rosy cheeks and a heavy dark fringe, and she succeeded in momentarily revolutionising the atmosphere of the schoolroom. She would say to the astonished governess 'Now then, Duckie-pie, we won't have his-try today; we'll have Gog-raphy', and Cark was so taken aback that she acquiesced. We worked out a good plan too, Stella and I, for halving the home-work, as there were certain books, scripture for instance, written in question-and-answer form and we would decide who was to start the allotted page as we were expected to begin at the beginning and answer the questions in turn though it was never stipulated who was to begin. It was some time before Cark tumbled to what was happening, but one awful day she looked suspiciously good-tempered and turned to me with the first question, saying, before either of us had time to reply, 'now, Sybil, *you* answer this one'. It was not the one I had learnt and I had no reply whatever to give. I don't remember the immediate consequences and I think probably owing to the presence of the Rosy-cheeked One the unfortunate incident was glossed over. I wonder now whether the child's departure had not something to do with the definite but imperceptible feeling of insubordination which was creeping into the schoolroom.

Boy, if I remember rightly, had about this time been sent off as a weekly boarder to the Cathedral preparatory school in a neighbouring town, often spending the weekends in my uncle's house on the outskirts of the town. Years later Aunt Jessie told me that his nervousness and repression at that time (the result of Cark's regime) was commented upon. The Head's wife tentatively asked her whether the boy had ever been ill treated at home. However, that phase passed; I am doubtful whether fundamentally one ever entirely frees oneself from the effects of early treatment, but he did well and normally at school and College and was keen on games & sports and in a general way was very popular. *Au fond* I still resent Cark more for her treatment of him than of me; in spite of the lasting effect it had on my attitude to life. Now that Cark felt herself less completely in control I believe she allowed herself less than ever the occasional moments of softness which had been possible when the parents were away. From the time they came home she seemed less sure of herself and less all-powerful though at the time I would have found it hard to explain the difference. She tried to take on almost the attitude of an elder daughter, making herself useful about the house, doing the flowers, and interesting herself in village occupations, as when for the visit of the Bishop I remember she made (and our help was requisitioned) numberless huge pink paper roses which, with a background of laurels, were to cover the archway made by the village carpenter to span the single street of the village.

Probably my mother was too—shall I say bewildered at the increase in her family & the difference of running a household in England after all the years in India to remonstrate adequately to control the situation. Contrary I believe to her doctor's advice she was expecting another baby (the fifth) and was always very occupied with the little sister having been used to her ways and in spite of her love for us two no doubt found it strangely difficult under the circumstances to get to know children of eight and nine with a background of repressions hard to penetrate. I know that she told one of the few people in whom she ever confided that she still had a special corner in her heart for her first baby, and that whatever I might take it into my head to do she felt certain that this would always be so. She was under no illusions about my body however, and when years later someone told her I was growing rather pretty, 'nonsense' said my mother firmly, 'she was always far too much like me ever to be pretty'.

Various visitors came to stay but they loom rather distant and unapproachable in my mind & I didn't see much of them except on Sundays when we were on show in white dresses and Eton suit. I remember particularly the visit of an Uncle and Aunt from Cornwall, relations of my father's first wife. He was stout and jovial with bushy eyebrows, a deep booming voice and a loud laugh which he followed up by slapping his knee and chuckling at his own jokes under the approving eye of his quiet and gentle wife. They had had one child only—a son who was coddled and fussed over so that it was a wonder he grew up as normally as he did. I can remember discussion before a dance he was to go to (this was of course some years later than the visit from which I have digressed!). Vividly I remember my Uncle's perturbation as to whether the boy was to wear a summer or a winter vest and the pros and cons of the Hot Ballroom versus facing the doubtful prospect of the elements on his Walk Home. Colds and Draughts were

86

considered with the utmost gravity and the return journey won the day. He probably spent the evening feeling like a hot house plant. I also remember that he was at one time not allowed to make a proposed voyage because it was impossible to get Grade A milk on board. This stuck in my mind as 'Gray Day' milk and I wondered what special properties it might have!

At one time Moira, the daughter of other old Army friends, the MacArthurs, came to stay. She was a lovely girl and certainly knew it as she repeated to me a remark which had been made in her hearing, batting her eyelids in the most approved style: 'That child could never be anything but beautiful with those eyes'. She was just my age and had in addition to the eyes masses of long and lovely brown hair, and behaved like an angel in public, but behind the scenes she sat on my back and pulled out my hair which was very fine and soft so that I could ill spare any, and it was to say the least painful. There were also two elderly sisters who impressed me when they came as being, to my childish sense, unusual; they were quiet and grey-haired and very gentle, and were distant cousins of ours. I remember hearing that they were psychic though I was of course considered too young to be interested in such things; but they struck me as being particularly simple, charming and different from anyone else I had ever known. They had wished for a dog and were given one of Bet's puppies (illegitimate but intelligent) and christened him Pompey. I was told that when one of the sisters died several years later, the remaining one declared that her sister often visited her, & that Pompey was conscious of these visits, at first objecting and his hair bristling as he whined & growled, but in the end he quietened down and wagged his tail. I never saw either of the sisters again and am not sure who told me this rather strange story.

I can't remember at all what servants we had at this period, but have a vague impression of innocuous & banal maids (no friends of ours). The only outstanding figure is that of a French cook, whose kitchen was her royaume and it was more than our life was worth to show a nose round the door unless specially invited. We might not even make much scuffling outside the door which opened from her kitchen onto the passage leading to the back stairs. Difficult, as we were entirely dependent on those stairs and on the passage as exit, the front of the house both in the hall and on the top landing being entirely cut off by double baize doors (what a delightfully quiet life our elders must have had in those days). It was arranged that the housework, except for bedrooms, was done almost entirely before breakfast, the maids getting up about 6.00 or 6.30 I think. One never saw maids about the house & passages & on the days when one particular room was 'turned out', it was done most discreetly—no fuss or noise of hoovers! There were high back stairs & passages & servants' hall too so plenty of room for the maids to have their own privacy.

I remember once falling over a brass coal scuttle when rushing down this dark passage & getting the full force of the blow just below the ribs. The wind was completely knocked out of me & I felt it for days, though I never dared admit my misdemeanours and no one apparently noticed anything amiss.

A small brother was born about this time, & was a very delicate little baby which was a grief & worry to my mother. She was snowed under with minor household worries and must have been on the verge of a breakdown. I had been turned out of the night nursery to make place for the new arrival and a stern sallow-faced woman who may have been an excellent nurse, but who to my recollection never smiled. I moved along the passage for a while, & was finally promoted to a room over the other side of the baize door in the front of the house. My impression of the christening is of Sunday clothes, and only the very long & voluminous lace-trimmed robe of the infant in the arms of the grey-clad sallow-faced nurse stands out from a small crowd of God-parents and others.

The baby only survived a few months; he was always ailing and died suddenly to my mother's great grief. The death of the other baby, Ruth, in India before Bunda's arrival had been a great shock to her & now the death of this child brought it all back with disastrous results to her health. I was impressed perhaps only with a general sadness, and yet I think with rather more than that for it was my first experience of Death so near at hand. I didn't see the dead baby, as Mother told me she would rather I remembered him as he had been and I readily left it at that. Poor little pinched face! but to my mother he had been her baby.

One day she had come out into the garden, and we were

sitting in the hazel arbour when she sent me to get a biscuit for the small sister and asked me whether I'd like one myself. I said 'no', feeling that a treat at that moment was out of place, and went off to find one for Bunda in the biscuit box which I knew always stood in the dining room—my resistance crumbled at the sight of the biscuits and on impulse I took one for myself too. How small things like that can remain in one's memory! I was filled with shame when, as I returned with two biscuits, I found my mother crying quietly. Though always for me someone quite apart—I didn't of course really know or understand her, accepting and admiring only, without question—I felt for her unbounded respect and love: yes, love—for though love can, through intimate knowledge, include all the attributes and peculiarities of an individual, one can also love very deeply an ideal. Yet such was my inability to express all the feeling which came flooding in that I couldn't throw my arms round her as I wanted to. I was too ashamed of my greed in taking the biscuit which had been offered me. And of course she couldn't have known how that long-legged inarticulate daughter of hers felt about it all.

Geraldine, our almost-grown-up cousin came to stay for a few days—to keep us occupied and out of the way I suppose. She had a great dramatic sense and on the day of the baby's funeral, taking us into the orchard where from higher ground we could see over the laurel hedge of the kitchen garden, she gave us a running commentary on the sad little procession such as one might get on the television in these days, and whether I really saw the minute white coffin on the knees of black-draped women in the covered carriage as they set off for the churchyard I couldn't say.

Dora took over the running of the household (Fra was still at college) and before long, we moved to another house, the Halesend, a delightful place, bright and comfortable with good open views. We led the open air and very free country life of those days in England, making many friends within a radius of about ten miles, & for us children there was much to explore and we knew every lane, wood and hillside path for miles round. My father & Dora rode a lot, and hunted regularly, and Cark was still with us though she doesn't to my recollection seem to have had such unlimited authority as before

89

except strictly in the schoolroom. My father didn't live very long & it must have been about two years later that he became very ill. We seldom saw him latterly, but I remember his nurse —a dark little woman who was friendly and kind to us, and used to come for walks in the woods and search even in those winter months for stray primroses. When they knew that the end was near, Bunda and I were sent over to Aunt Jessie at The Elms, about sixteen miles away, which in those days was quite a distance & had to be undertaken by train. It was to the Cathedral school there that Michael had been sent as a weekly boarder, & he often spent week-ends up at this house which stood on a hill overlooking the town. Before leaving we went up to my father's room to say goodbye, and I have a very clear picture of him in his dressing-gown sitting in a big chair in front of the fire looking terribly ill and frail. He was very gentle with us and though we had been told nothing I realized without a question that it was for the last time. I was absolutely miserable at The Elms and hated being there but I think it was only a few days before the news came that Father was dead. My cousin looked upon us rather like live dolls, and with her usual dramatic sense enjoyed dressing us both in black and curling our hair no doubt with great effect as I remember her pleasure at the interest shown by neighbours in 'the pretty little cousins'.

Unk had come South for the funeral & came over especially to see us and I couldn't bear the thought of meeting him in the atmosphere of that household, so very different from his own and antagonistic to all my recollections of him. My feelings were I think from any reasonable point of view unjustifiable for my aunt was kindness itself in her practical and rather worldly-wise way, but I always felt like a fish out of water in that entourage. I went and hid in the immense garden under some thick bushes, and only came out unwillingly when I could no longer pretend to be unconscious of the search. I know I longed to throw my arms round my Uncle's neck as in the old days, and I've often wondered whether he understood my silent unhappiness. I think he did, for after he left I was at once for no apparent reason sent home & I remember Dora putting her arms round me when I arrived (they were kindly & very well-meaning arms but never motherly) and

90

asking me why I hadn't said I didn't want to go away. I still said nothing—what could I have said? I had never been asked.

There were other visits to The Elms less disastrous, but curiously enough I never really felt at home there. Two big deer hounds (Rhanee and Prince) lived in the house & were remarkably decorative and beautiful. On one of my visits, there were three or four puppies almost as large as the parents, and when I was sent out into the garden with my mid-morning biscuits and chocolate they all came bounding towards me with incredible swiftness and greeted me with an exuberance which—as they were all capable of putting large paws on my shoulders & towering over me while administering hearty licks—rather frightened me, and throwing my biscuits to the winds, I fled. By the time the last biscuit had disappeared, I was well within doors! A very nervous red-roan pony, Lady-bird (black mane and tail), was always used in the trap for station work, local shopping and visits, often two or three times a day. She was driven by a very correct and red-faced groom in uniform, and he seemed to have her well under control, but she was never still a minute and I doubt whether she would have been very manageable in any other hands. She was very restless and had a particularly quick trot so that her hooves clattered gaily and seemed hardly to touch the ground as she went spanking along her head held superbly & her fine action very effective. In the stables (or rather in a loft over the stables) lived a stray Manx cat who was a great friend of mine & I often visited him taking very special care to avoid Ladybird's heels on the way up the ladder. My uncle had retired from the army some years before & the household was when I first knew it already well-established, impeccably run, and both my Uncle and Aunt were active on the Hospital Board and various local Committees, and of course in those days of 'calling' there was a continuous and active social life.

The house was very large, perfect for entertaining. The big music-room had a raised stage at one end & an excellent dancing floor & seemed even larger than it was because of huge mirrors at the far end. The grounds too were ideal for theatricals, garden parties & such like entertainments, though it was only some years later that I began to appreciate this. I am not sure how many rooms there were, but there certainly must have been eight bedrooms at least, and about the same number of living rooms quite apart from the servants' quarters. There were several men employed and six or seven maids apart from daily char women. The servants' quarters were entirely apart down a large back passage and looked out onto a small courtyard and the stables & coach house. After my father's death, my uncle became our Guardian. I always found him quite unapproachable, severe and forbidding in manner though always strictly polite. He seldom appeared except at meals, and I can't remember his ever speaking directly with me. I believe he had a very violent temper when young and I was told that when he married my aunt (fresh from a Convent school) she went through periods when he would lock himself in his room and refuse to talk to her! They had three children. I hardly knew the youngest boy, 'Frog', who was delicate & died when just grown-up. The eldest son Morris was in the army, & the girl Geraldine was the only one with whom I often came in contact. Francie had been more or less brought up with Geraldine while our parents were in India (Dora had gone out with them) and this household was a second home to her. I on the other hand felt strange and lost and never entirely got over this. I was always like a fish out of water & longed for my familiar & less sophisticated surroundings.

The next few months are very vague in my mind, but it was not long after the baby's death that my mother had a complete nervous and mental breakdown, and was sent to a nursing home. Apart from the fact that we were told she would soon be home again, a curtain was dropped. The doctors were in fact hopeful. There were good periods and relapses. Had she been treated with the experience and knowledge of mental trouble gained *entre deux guerres* there is every probability that all would have righted itself. I was told years later that it had been suggested that she might come home with nurses, but the move was not made and months and years passed. We were told very little and never encouraged to speak of her. So she became a Shadow, and I never saw her again till I was grown up. By that time it was too late even to hope, had there been any hope. Her husband was dead, their son killed in action, and there were no threads she could have picked up, but it was many years before she was laid beside my father in the country churchyard on the hill. What endless misunderstandings in our intimate relationships and even real unhappiness can be caused by the systematic suppression of thoughts

Dora Hewat

and feelings. It can engender finally an almost fierce refusal to face discussion for fear of contradiction or the shattering of fundamental ideas, and may take years to overcome. Though children are very open to reason, it is terribly easy to bottle them up, and unless they can discuss or talk things over with someone whose character and conception of life can meet their own beliefs and imaginings on common ground the result is usually silence.

93

'Hullo! Adams—not paid for your boots yet?' I can still see the scene. A summer morning full of subtle sounds and smells such as town dwellers know nothing of, and we were all in our places round the dining room table for breakfast. The 'grown ups' and two friends, myself, my brother, the small sister and her governess. It was a large room; two french windows opened onto a stretch of lawn and at the far end of the room was a sideboard which I always picture laden with food although our household was a simple one for those pre-1914 days. There was usually a huge ham and a choice of kippers, sausage, bacon & eggs or perhaps fish cakes, and everyone helped himself. Dora at the end of the table poured out tea. The wretched Adams was a school friend of Michael's, invited for the holidays and meeting the family for the first time. We never waited for late comers before starting breakfast, & there was a moment of expectancy when the door opened slowly and Adams appeared, obviously quaking in his shoes (or boots) and not quite sure of the best procedure.

The atmosphere was somewhat casual, & after a nodded greeting he was told to help himself at the sideboard. He was extremely shy & had a quiet manner, and in the silence which had fallen on his entry he made his way across what must have seemed an interminable stretch of carpet. The only sound was the creaking of his new shoes & Dora's query reduced the poor boy to stammering apologies while he blushed to the roots of his hair and rather large ears. I think Dora was probably unconscious of the effect of her remark & quite genuinely meant to put him at his ease! but it was only after a hearty breakfast that he began to recover his usual quiet and rather charming manner and probably enjoyed the rest of his visit, for we were a young crowd and there was always plenty to do in summer and winter alike. The description of the house which follows may sound complicated but I risk giving it as the general set-up was unusually pleasant. I should suggest that if you are not interested either in domestic architecture or in hide-and-seek you should skip a bit!

The house was large, square and white, the walls rose and jasmine-covered up to the top floor level. It had been built by a man who, being afraid of fire, had insisted on having double doors between each room both upstairs and down. So it was, for a young family, the most ideal place for hide-and-seek and a variety of games in the dark with a luminous match-box. Each room opened into the hall (or upstairs onto the landing) & connected also through double doors with the next room; and there was ample space to hide between each pair of double doors. One could in this way go right round the house without emerging into the hall or landing, and whichever room one hid in there were at least two exits so the chases were complicated and exciting.

Standing in the hall with one's back to the front door the stairs were directly in front of one, and at the far end of the hall a door led to the back premises. The schoolroom (the only room with only one door & which therefore we always used as 'home') was on the left, and the drawing room door on the right, then through double doors into the dining rooms, & across to more double doors leading into the morning room, which in turn opened both into the greenhouse and into the back hall with a pantry and side entrance. From there one could pass back into the hall and the front of the house and the third door led to the kitchen premises which were completely self-contained but usually voted out of bounds; a large kitchen, hall & back door, a scullery, larder & another side door leading into a yard. These two back exits led onto a stretch of rough grass beyond which were the stables. There were back stairs to the servants' rooms, bathroom and top landing. It was a house intended for a large family and servants with comfortable space for both, and yet not rambling or full of passages & dark corners as are so many old houses. The cellars, coalhole, potting shed etc. were all there but could be ignored, & there were also good stables & loft.

The house stood high and well away from the narrow lane which ran past unseen on a lower level, being in a dip between the sloping garden and flat open fields. It was surrounded by garden and a wilderness bordering the drive, though the immediate surroundings of the house were open and sunny with a view right out over the fields and an enormous copper beech to one side, its branches sweeping the ground & leaving a real garden house for children underneath, out of sight and with climbing possibilities to keep them occupied for many hours. The kitchen garden was behind the house on a higher level, & beyond that a disused quarry & hill-side, woods and fields.

There were often gypsy encampments within a few miles so that gypsies used occasionally to come begging. They could always have something to eat & a cup of soup or tea but were never given money. Even so one had to insist that they eat whatever they took before leaving, or they were apt to waste large slices of bread & butter or even cheese or meat, simply throwing it away as they were not hungry & only anxious for cash.

In early days pocket money could be earned by black-berrying, weeding and fruit-picking, 6d. an hour, and was usually spent in the very small post-office-cum-General-Stores at Stifford's Bridge about ten minutes' walk away over the fields, where one could rely on finding a good supply of chocolate and boiled sweets of virulent colours. It was perhaps just as well that one or two of these sweets were enough to make one feel sick so that one was not tempted to be too extravagant! A large square yard in front of the post office was once a year given over to hurdy-gurdies but it was very rough and I don't remember ever being allowed to go; the distant refrain 'when we are married we'll have sausages for tea' reached us clearly over the fields & rang in my ears for days at a time. At that time & for several years we were very much 'in the schoolroom' and in bed by 7.30. (The various memories of this house stretch over a good many years—in all from when I was ten until I came back from Germany when I was seventeen.)

Animals were inevitable. The dogs usually mongrels, intelligent and devoted, and there was a miscellaneous collection of hens & rabbits who lived together in an enclosure of rough grass near the stables. At first we still had Bet, the brown and white spaniel with sex appeal & frequent families. One of her puppies, Boodles (black and white) was a friend over many years, and once when an enquiring visitor wanted to know what sort of dog it was, the small sister firmly replied that 'he had been trained to be a spaniel'. There was Jack too who with a stretch of the imagination might have been taken for a

Michael at The Halesend with Jack & Boodles

rough haired terrier. These two found by experience that it was hard work digging to get below the netting which surrounded the rabbit enclosure & was well embedded in the ground, but one day they hit upon a bright idea. They dug fairly deep holes outside the netting, the rabbits watching; then they went away to a distance and awaited events. Sure enough the rabbits completed the burrow from their side and emerged for a short and succulent meal on the grass before the chase began. Fortunately they were in full view of the kitchen window—and as far as I remember the dogs after that concluded that the result of the scheme was unsatisfactory.

A much later addition after I went to school was a bulldog which Fra acquired. I remember her sitting quite happily with an undercurrent of growling going on, the Bulldog on one side of her chair and Jack, hair bristling and teeth showing, growling from the other side; I was frankly terrified of the bulldog, and these rumblings and sudden bursts of ill concealed

97

canine fury, even if they led to nothing very serious, were always imminent and disturbing.

There were a number of grass snakes about & I remember that once, having tried to kill one with a stick, I dropped him in a bucket of water (for safety's sake, I thought) whereupon he revived and made good his escape. I must have had it in me to be a perfect pest in some ways, and I remember once running after Fra holding a grass snake by the tail, a thing I would certainly be incapable of doing now. Wet or fine we children spent most of our time out of doors and I think that the grown-ups did too, though blazing open fires were always in evidence if anyone wanted them.

In those days we always dressed for dinner at 7.30. My sisters were both lovely girls, & Dora looked particularly striking as I remember in a black velvet dress; *décolleté* and touching the ground. I thought her the more beautiful of the two with her deep brown and naturally wavy hair. Fra was the more spectacular. Fair, very well built and tall she would sail into a room taking it by storm, with masses of fair hair and a complexion which took one's breath away. I was frankly plain, and usually wore white, or a blue velvet dress with an Irish lace collar, my hair tied back with a large black bow. My brother Michael always put on an Eton suit which suited him well. Bunda was by that time already in bed. It was a habit after dinner to play cards, but as I hated this I finally gave it up, & used to read or sew instead. We continually had visitors; friends of our own age or friends of my sisters' as well as relatives. I can't say there were many intellectual pursuits (or did they pass me by?) nor were ideas or the art of interesting conversation encouraged in our family as one gathers was to some extent the case in previous generations in England.

The advent of Adams with his boots was of course later than many of the adventures I have described but I think they give an idea of the surroundings in which he found himself. We had a very good hard tennis court in a clearing amongst the trees, riding for the equestrian-minded, and a pony trap to get into the neighbouring town four miles away. I say pony trap but the animal was really a cob from Ireland, strong & active, and we thought nothing of a day's expedition to watch county cricket or to go to the roller skating rink, either of which entailed doing ten miles each way. We had a passion at one time for roller-skating, and I can still remember the thrill of movement and the swing of skates to the tune of a band in what seemed a vast hall. On these occasions we hailed the ostler in the yard of the Red Lion and had the pony fed and put up until we were ready to start home again.

In hard winters we skated on a square pond below the house and often spent most of the day there, with biscuits, ginger snaps and cups of hot chocolate in the middle of the morning. In that pond lived the largest gold fish I have ever seen. He was fat and (this is not a tall story) well over a foot in length! I suppose he dug himself into the mud when the pond iced over, for he always reappeared with the thaw, and lived there all the years that I knew the house, though he looked after himself entirely and seemed to thrive in his lonely splendour.

In summer we had a fine cricket pitch at the far end of the lawn, and cricket was, as I remember it, the favourite occupation, though as we got older tennis took up a lot of our time, and we became reasonably efficient. We used to get up cricket matches 'grown-ups versus children', collecting our teams from willing neighbours within a seven miles radius. Some played quite well, & it was amusing to see the boys crowd in for catches as soon as the grown-ups took bat in hand. I had been known to get some good catches in slips so was often placed there, but personally preferred to field well away from the wicket, so that I had plenty of time to see the ball coming! The lawn must have been large as we seldom lost a ball or did any damage though there were dense rhododendrons, firs and beech trees in one direction and in the other a large greenhouse, not to speak of the five french windows of the house which opened onto this lawn.

John, the gardener, managed the whole place including a large kitchen garden with the help of a boy, & very occasionally the groom lent a hand, but he had his own very definite ideas about a garden and if he said that a plant was not suitable one might give up all idea of having it, as it would never be allowed to grow. He was quite a character, & I can't picture the place without him pottering around. He lived with his wife in a two storeyed cottage under the hill behind the house (I remember that the rent was £10 a year) and she always came and did the laundry two days a week. She was a tiny woman, always bright and smiling—he taciturn but very kindly at heart, good natured and utterly reliable. They had come to us at the first house, were with us for nearly twenty years & saw us through three moves. On wet days John always enjoyed being in the potting shed and greenhouse and was never idle—slow, but sure! He had a great array of potted plants in the greenhouse which didn't appeal to me at all, but of which he was inordinately proud. Three plants I remember as being very lovely. They were well established over years, growing from under foot—an asparagus fern covering a whole wall, a flourishing vine, and another wall covered by a particularly beautiful pure white rose rather wax-like and lovely when in bud, drooping when in full bloom and hanging heavily amongst delicately pale green foliage. It was a rose I've never seen since.

We had no motor mower; and it is only now in thinking of that well-kept lawn with surprise that my memory is jogged & I hear distinctly 'clop, clop'—and see Roween the pony turning the corner of the house led by Prince, the groom and shod with heavy leather boots (the like of which I've never seen since) to prevent her damaging the grass. She didn't much like the feel of those boots and lifted each foot high 'clop, clop, clop' in unmistakeable protestation. The three would then methodically set about cutting the lawn, Roween led by the groom while old John guided the heavy mower. Only the grass beyond the lawn and amongst the trees was allowed to grow long, and scythed from time to time.

That countryside holds so many memories and I knew all the woods, hedges and ditches & every flower likely to be found for miles round except in the direction of the village which was more civilized & didn't interest me so much, though it was a lovely village—black and white timbered cottages & the village Stores, the church and churchyard dominated the scene on rising ground above & as it were keeping an eye on all the comings and goings in the winding lane which ran through.

There were several hunts in the neighbourhood and Dora was an excellent horsewoman & hunted regularly on her horse

'The Grey' but my pony was too excitable for me to enjoy when the hounds were about. I had no qualms as to the ethics of hunting in those days and we'd follow for miles on foot though fortunately for me I was never in at a kill. The foxes were very numerous and clever and nine times out of ten they got away to my entire satisfaction. My outstanding impression is of sunshine, scarlet coats, the intermittent sound of the horn, and the hounds scattering over the hills.

They were happy care-free days in the holidays, though term time banished us from all this except at weekends. There was always for about a week before term began the inevitable nightmare sorting of clothes, darning, mending, & replacing any missing from the school list of necessities. How I hated the idea of school & though once there I had some quite happy times I always look back upon it as a hateful period. Even the holidays were rather overshadowed by 'holiday work' which had a habit of getting put off till the last moment & was often very dull I thought. *Bleak House* for instance had once to be waded through—& left no lasting impression—but I found it interminable. I think that in comparison with continental Education (though I don't pretend to have gone into the subject thoroughly) the training of the young in England has been and is less thorough and indeed very insular and haphazard—but it seems to have its advantages & is for its individual character-forming qualities preferable to the intense grind which is too frequent on the Continent. I believe (& hope) all the same that this has considerably altered since my time & education is taken more seriously!

On the hillside above the house stood a pollarded willow with a huge hollow space amongst the branches into which if agile one could climb. One was completely invisible but through the branches shooting up all round one there was a view of the whole country-side for miles—a wonderful vantage point where I often used to settle myself with a book for hours at a time.

Then there was the woodpecker's tree in the orchard beyond a disused quarry. They nested there every year having pecked a neat round hole in the trunk of an old apple tree. It was too small even for children's hands to penetrate! but one could hear the family chirping deep down in the trunk, and

101

Pencil drawing by Sybil

watch the parent birds coming to and fro if one sat in the spinney a few yards away—a tangle of undergrowth, carpeted in spring with primroses and wild daffodils, & in this field such treasures as butterfly and bee orchises could occasionally be found. There were of course nests of all sorts, and the rabbit population was innumerable. From my tree I often watched whole families playing and rolling about like puppies below me. There was a fir tree not far off which I used to climb if feeling very adventurous, but that was a very tall tree and a real climbing feat; then too, one came down with one's hair full of twigs looking rather like a hedgehog I imagine. Not very popular or to be encouraged!

Above the quarry there was a good point of view from which, when my brother came back from school filled with enthusiasm about morse code, he used to signal with a white flag to the opposite hillside where I had to take up position, decipher the messages and send suitable replies with a white flag, an entertainment which kept us busy for hours. Little did I think that thirty years or so later I should climb that same hill with my husband and lie amongst the primroses in the flickering sunshine of the coppice which bordered the hill top!

Another favourite occupation was to organize paper-chases which entailed climbing over stiles & walking for miles over fields and woods of which I knew every inch, and along lanes usually bordered by high banks & hedges. It was very varied hilly country, and these lanes in spring were thickly lined with primroses and violets (white as well as purple), in summer with wild roses and honeysuckle, and in the winter we splashed through untold mud in an effort to keep up with the boys. Adams was at least lucky to be a summer visitor, as he avoided the mud which to town-dwelling friends must have been horrifying though it is only when I look back on those days that I realize how particularly all-pervading and inescapable it was, probably owing to the high banks which allowed water to flow between them or to lie in muddy puddles of unusual size barring the way to any but the most intrepid adventurers.

Another memory of that house is in the hop-picking season, when the smell of hops was everywhere. Below the stables and seen from the back of the house was a large gate

Portrait of Sybil by Melton Fisher (detail), 1926
He was her teacher at the Slade.

Sybil, photographed by Anne at the period when she
was writing her memoirs. Ardennes, Summer, 1964

opening out onto farm buildings; and away beyond this gate a huge open barn. Each year the pickers, sent down from large cities & of course bringing children and babies with them, were allowed to camp in this barn & in the evenings used to light a huge fire in the open space in front. They would sit and stand about in the flickering light and sing songs or dance round the fire. It was an enthralling *scène de théâtre* for us as we watched them in the uncertain light while they sang choruses late into the night.

*   *   *   *

The line on the map has become hills, trees,
a place, not a direction. The lines of her memoir
merge into realities, a white house,
my life overlapping hers across seventy years.
I check all the details, and find everything,
except the pollarded willow in whose giant cup,
running over with light, she escaped the world—
and found it, looking through the long shoots
into the distance. Rotted by too many rains,
the tree is gone, and I have only myself
to hold, for an afternoon, to this overflow,
a spring light such as I know she loved.
There is a smell of early hay, black earth
breathes through the long grasses and has risen,
delicate, through wild rose and harebell.

Housman came here, in memory of a lad
who lived in this house before my mother came,
and killed himself for loss of the vicar's daughter.
Cradley churchyard commemorates him and Michael,
sons of The Halesend who died too young,
though in different wars. Housman praised him,
knowing that a soul undone may undo others.
      Shot? So quick, so clean an ending?
      Oh that was right, lad, that was brave:
      Yours was not an ill for mending,
      'Twas best to take it to the grave.
Brave. But bravest, best? More difficult,
anyway, the etceteras of survival,
the surprise of finding love beyond love's end.

I talk with the daughter of the house. We stand
together under the copper beech and she shows me,
here, how a branch curves to a child-sized seat.
She used to be swung in it so that the sun dazzled
through the dark dome.
               I remind myself
how far apart we might have seemed, she and I,
meeting elsewhere. And from under the day's brightness
slides that social shadow which would have divided me

107

from grandmother, mother, Michael. Possession, dispossession,
love unoffered across so many frontiers, not least
those of politics in the name of humanity.
                                        We walk across
the perfect lawn to the tea-table, still set where I know,
from photographs, my mother's family gathered
on long summer evenings before the first world war.
There is nothing here to waken unkindness.
We talk of the record that garden and house afford
of owners come and gone over centuries,
additions, removals, alterations. I feel myself afloat
on circumstance, as they were, a living core
strangely unchanging from one life to another,
the past, today, the future, beyond love's end.

In the churchyard, the daisies lean to the light,
the long grass has been scythed and left lying.
Nothing is easy. The dead, whatever the living feel,
lie dead.
          Even so, overflowing
our own deaths too, a tide that should be of darkness
spreads out beyond all this into shining reaches.

*   *   *   *

Cradley Churchyard from near the Hewat memorial
Photographed by Anne, Summer, 1980

LETTERS FROM MICHAEL TO HIS SISTER SYBIL, FROM FRANCE

13.1.15

We were near a village which had been badly shelled yesterday.
I have never seen such a sight. Practically every house was
utterly ruined—tremendous shell-holes in the road. I had a
look at the church—a small one—no roof & very little wall
standing—pieces of stained glass, images, broken pillars lying
about everywhere, and the graveyard was all ploughed up by

Jack Johnsons. An officer there who had been right through this show said he had never seen anything like it.

Just after we left the Germans put some more shells into it, but I don't think they could have done more damage.

It is extraordinary how comfortable the men make themselves with no materials for doing so. Those in my lot boiled themselves several brews of tea, the only fuel being G.S. biscuit.

18.1.15

Had my first experience of decent shelling the day before yesterday, when we went up about a mile and a half behind the firing line on a fatigue. Everybody was working away merrily when we heard the whistle of a shell coming. You could see everybody crouching down. It came down about 30 yards in front of us. It was so unexpected that everyone stood up and roared with laughter. However when they heard a second one coming they fairly ran for cover. None of our party was hit except R.E.'s who were knocked down by large clods of earth which descended on them.

24.1.15

Trenches in a more or less collapsible condition. The first shell which burst 500 yards off knocked a large wet & heavy sandbag on my head, resulting in the loss of my second service cap, and a net gain of about a ton & a half of mud. Had bad weather there, first rain then hard frost, but worked it in twelve hour reliefs, so that had quite a good time. When not in trenches we were in a house just behind called Dead Cow House. The smell of it was the limit outside but curiously enough was alright when you got right in—not comfortable, but quite safe, as the smell though not shell & bullet proof was calculated to keep the King's enemies at a distance.

Very few casualties except through sickness owing to water in the trenches.

110

6.2.15

Now in a very famous part of the line.

Not a moment to write as I am left senior subaltern of the Corps. I am in charge at the moment. However I suppose I shall have to hand over when another Captain turns up. They may not be able to find one though. A lot of shells knocking round. We are quartered in a large red brick building of 3 storeys—rather an attractive mark for artillery. The Officers' quarters are in what was rather a nice private house. The Germans have bust open the safe, & left empty jewel cases scattered all over the place. A lovely piano—beautifully toned —also plenty of comfortable chairs. Everything just as they left it except for being bust about. Scrap books, family photos etc. all lying about. Plenty of crockery, which we use.

Have just had an order to proceed to another job—meant to write a decent letter—will manage to do so some day.

19.2.15

Billets. Back here for forty eight hours now; we do 48 in the trenches then 48 in reserve & so on ad infinitum. At present no one is allowed on leave as we are in a very important spot & everybody is frightfully scared that the Germans are going to try & break through here. I expect we shall have a long rest when we are finished here.

The billets are very nice. I get a bath whenever I come down here, & there is an arm chair—a very rare thing in France.

27.2.15

Your guess was more or less correct except that the place you mention is two miles inside the German lines. I couldn't face the vermi-something Dora sent. The horrors of war aren't quite as bad as that stuff. Thank her for the chocolate and ginger. The Officers are beginning to get leave now. Two from this Battalion got 8 days' leave yesterday.

Dear Syb.

Thanks for your letter. The place you mentioned in your first letter was not the same as the one in your second!!! So I suppose you had forgotten which place you did mention. Nothing much doing here at present. We have been back for a day this time. We go up tomorrow and come back again, probably, in a couple of days, for some time. When next you are in Hereford could you get me a packet of 'Gillette' safety blades, half a dozen for 2p, which will last me for a long time. The photos are in a parcel ready to be sent back with the first person who goes on leave. You should not show them to too many people. Please thank somebody very much for the magazines etc. which arrived yesterday and we got them this morning when we came out of the trenches. Will write again soon—when we get back. Love to the Family.

Yrs.
Miggs.

P.S. You might ask Dora to let me know what that tailor's bill was and I will send her a cheque for it.

[This was Michael's last letter from the front. He was killed on this sortie, on the next day (March 10). The 'Dora' mentioned in the footnote is, of course, his sister Dora.]

*   *   *   *

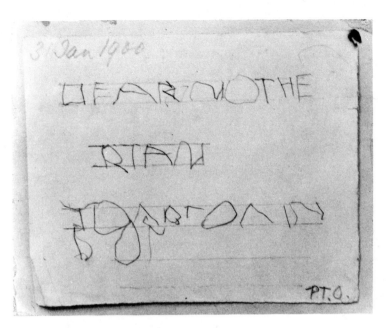

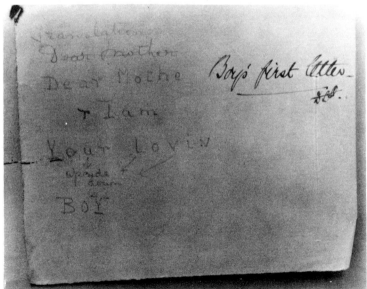

Michael's first letter to his mother. It reads 'Dear Mother I am your loving Boy', with the 'l' and 'v' of 'loving' upside down. 31 Jan 1900.

Michael in uniform, 1914
Killed in action, 10 March 1915, aged nineteen

The front, 3 Feb. 1915, near Givenchy. Taken by Michael.

View from Woodend, taken by Anne, 1980.

On the skyline beyond our stream those trees,
they say, mark graves long vanished,
the stones gone to make gate-posts,
flesh and bones gone to seed, reaped.
Maybe they're all forgotten, though I doubt it.
Someone, somewhere, turns up a tiny box
of rusted icing, like this one here,
or photographs of legendary folk, whose traits
said to live on in child or grandchild now
emerge for good or ill in the new born.
I haven't met the people who might remember.
But these, these relics, my own history,
brown photos of the dead, the shaky outline
of baby's foot, aged one (my mother's),
a pressed leaf, letters not telling much,
one even now unopened, sixty years later—
affections echoed before I lived to feel them—
these mark the secret ground of a shared life.

Looking across, how secret the change is!
My skyline echoes a strange outline,
a churned slope up to a clump of trees
near Givenchy, 1915. The eyes that framed it
become my eyes, our trees look shell-blasted.
After his death in March, after the last censored
humorous teenage letters in pencil arrived,
came these photographs, his last message
to the younger sisters who had romped with him
in trees and on rivers that 1914 summer.
Much older than uncle was, I'm as little able
to say what I see in this skyline. But now
I do understand my mother's eye for details,
the scarlet pimpernel, the four leafed clover,
chestnut buds tacky in mid-winter,
things one remembers seeing a first time.
There's a shadow of communion in them, memory
makes them appear the same instead of new,
re-newed, as the seasons overlay each other.
A secret language of the eye, censored
by custom if we try to speak it, links us

with the dead, their strange reticences, politics,
no odder than ours to them. That muddied hillside,
this grassy slope: a riddle seen, not solved.
Somewhere, a primitive eye may search a skyline
not unlike this one, sharing in our silence.
The blood-red hands have so long reached up
to the cave's darkness, the mother's pencil
etched on a scrap of paper a tiny foot.

At the birth of my husband's mother, their Indian doctor
seeing at the bedside the toddler's fistful
of strange flowers, asked 'What has the little chap
got there?' 'I've brought daisies for my baby.'
'Then you must call her Daisy.' And they did.
Two generations later, that exchange is retold,
with love, exactly. The toddler and the doctor
are both dead, the baby well past seventy.
My stepchild Tim outlines his hand in biro.
After our deaths, those trees may catch his eye.
Affections share us, though we fail to name them,
and ground relations in more than relationship.

*   *   *   *

Michael with Monica ('Bunda'), Summer, 1914

118

*   *   *

Somewhere down the black hole
of memory, that bank of white
violets enjoys its shade, the funeral

of the boy killed on a tractor winds
through the village—'No, don't stare'
'Why?' 'It's not polite'—

and up the hill the young farmer
on the pony holds his superior nose
at my donkey, in the clear spring air.

It's a friendly signal, and we go
together in the pony-trap at tea-time
to milk the cows in the far meadow.

All of nine years old, I eat my jam
sandwich in the shade, concentrating
on its crisp edges. Older than I am

by all of six years, concentrating
on the milking, my friend tilts his back
to udder after udder, and the jets swing.

That was summer. In the different dark
of a winter's tea-time, the big shire,
almost on its knees, struggles to free the cart

from frozen mud, and in misplaced anger
I have grappled with my friend's whip arm.
The cart rolls back. All is to do over.

Other children, other times. Other harm.
Not so long after that, when the war
was over, I remember the hushed auditorium

of the local cinema, the sudden fear
of my father's hand over my eyes as the first
concentration-camp pictures were shown there.

Through his fingers, I saw the bodies thrust
before the bulldozer-scoop into the hole,
and a speechless survivor interviewed at the huts.

Years later, when I lifted a corrugated sheet
against a wall and found a man, bent double,
that hand over my eyes made me simply replace it—
that, and the milk's heart-beat filling the pail.

*   *   *

The knife reduces a polished oval
to mimosa on the chopping board.
Free of the shell, day-old chicks tumble

like mimosa from their box onto the floor.
Animated egg—egg sacrificed!
My mother, or myself, scraping the board.

Only some forty years divide
these women. Time enough for her
to die. Almost my whole life

so far. And then, how much further?
How keen and clear these seventeenth-century
broodings make each everyday pleasure,

Everywoman's task. Her hands were ugly
with domestic scars, by which I remember them now
(mine are less scarred, less gentle) most exactly.

As if on a desert island, she knew how
to make do. A harp made with string
and nails, from a fire-log, somehow

tuned to all the songs I wanted to sing
in the secret, sacred willow above the nettles,
where she pretended not to know I was hiding.

Making do. Making sacred. The magic spells
love works on coincidence. I don't need
to be told what that letter tells—

unanswerable, a friend's fatal disease.
These chores tell it all in miniature.
And what is missing, memory supplies.

Folded, unanswered, a white blur
on the table-top, it becomes part of our home,
the sign of another marriage in our décor.

Signs in each other's lives, across time
also, though not always recognized, keep faith.
I know now that my mother used to climb

such a secret tree, pollarded, springing. Faith
with that memory helped her to let me hide
despite 'lunch ready' (and the rest). Near-death
of a friend is now what I think of, turned aside.

*   *   *

The empty stairs from studio to studio
were frightening, even to a child,
wide, flat, marble-cold.

Dark, too, in the early day
when the lights in the high well
of the stair had turned pale.

Two or three at a time, from third floor
to ground, one at a time back
with the breakfast milk, I would stop to talk

with the small man from below,
floor two (the only talkative occupant),
in his dark velvet short-coat.

Invited into his studio for tea,
with my parents, I remember he'd lift
me chest high, in affection, to eat

my biscuit while he argued theories
of painting, lifting each dark oil
with his spare arm onto the easel.

Upstairs again, my mother would turn
the taps on the gas-jets and light
the fragile gauzes, easily damaged or burnt

to a black hole. Moving the goldfish
from the table, and laying the bright red
cloth for our family dinner, I wished

he wasn't down there below in a dark
I only imagined, a quiet I could not guess.
At an exhibition, the painted marks

above the long-unthought-of name
brought it all back: the slight dust over
everything, how a passing German bomber

blew my goldfish out of its bowl. I remember
all this, now, but for a moment the man
below has lost his name, and only the turn

of his arm about me, lifting, is perpetual.
I dedicate that nameless memory, as I remember
the man's name, to Yankel Adler.

*   *   *

The mountains outside have folded the snow
into miles of untouched brightness. How night
seems to hover up there amongst the slow,

slow stars, while down here there is snowlight!
Now a pigeon grumbles under the archway,
disturbed, as I am, tempted to flight.

I think the squabs, born too early, may
never fledge, never fly: the skin through which
guts and eyes show blue, not likely one day

to sprout the white cloak whose magic swish
would carry them up on summer winds, rising
to a view of the mountains, tippling almost to a smash.

While the snow, untouched between us, is lying
white over the moors, and the small claw marks
of grouse and mouse, or the rabbit's triads, fling

their delicate veins of passage between iced grasses—
whose blackened blades, against the light, sway and shine—
a vein of thoughts, too, lies delicate and passes

for silence, passes like snow into the soil. Then
new life grows, and those marks vanish for ever
into the moor. Memories seep down.

The snow lies untouched between us. A clear,
black, cold night hovers above the snow.
The pigeon settles to his nest. He'll rear

his squabs after all, maybe, to tipple in the blow
of this harsh place. Love's earlier passages
rest at the root of the slow, slow

magic that a good marriage is.
New life grows. The sensitive skin,
overlaying past lives, slowly fledges.

The night and the snow hold us all, in
a giant vault. Somewhere miles away
across the untouched brightness, loves lain

to rest, with their own memories delicately vein
the distance between us. You and I will wake
together, husband and wife, into our next day.

*   *   *

Jocund. Jocund. After such pleasures.
The coffee is cold, interrupted by
other more urgent homely matters.

You patter back from the bathroom, innocently
dangling, with a cloth and a warm towel,
and a kiss, taking good care of me.

Cold coffee, then, sitting up in the jewel
the sun makes of our unmade bed,
the ruby sheets holding our smell.

Husband and wife as Van Eyck painted
in no known canvas, but might have liked to,
judging by the tender picture that he made—

the hands' touch, the modest look
of true love about to happen,
the little dog not excluded, the pool

of the round mirror's limpid reflection,
hung on the wall like the eye of time
approving it all, the there and then

of chance affection, like the light come
to that window-sill from far away.
Infinite space left unlit for a little room.

This and that brought us this way,
personal decisions, political events,
chances that came to seem like fate.

Like fate, too, the coming bereavements,
illness, old age, death. Often now,
our present falters at presentiments.

To hold one another in the glow
of a moment's safety is the miracle
only life offers! What we know

of love, persuades that our trouble
binds us to someone's future happiness.
Our ancestors in darkness dwell

for ever, still, despite the happiness
their actions brought us to, this pool
of winter sun in which we dress.

*   *   *

Drawing the blinds, we two would romp
on all fours, wrapped in blankets,
in the dark, crying out '*C'est les phoques*

qui s'avancent, dit Gilbrand!' Parents
safely off somewhere, child and adult
would become seals in the wastes

of bedroom, stairs, cubby-hole, a rut
of monster beings, ourselves, pursuing—
in a dark made more familiar—us, us!

The cries echo. Your letters are telling,
now that we are both adult, a stranger
tale, of the mind slowly exploring

its own darkness, finding a secret door
that opens between the eyes on a breaking
ice-floe. You are my nurse no more.

In my own game, I still blunder
through too-well-known places, making
nonsense with noises, but a child no longer.

Just as I didn't know the source
of that childhood phrase, I cannot know,
now, the history of these words whose force

works, like magic, on the dark floe
of life. The voices that made
their sense for me are gone in the undertow.

To my thoughts, I welcome every shade
surviving from cave, desert, wood,
city, where those games were played.

The strange cries that change us could
be meaningless—but for that change.
In the dark night of a desperate mood

the artifice of a clarinet will change
death to life. The touch of a head
against ours, that we love, will change,

beyond our physics, what goes on inside.
More meaningless still than words, these strange
messages echo between us, heard and unheard.

*   *   *

RESTING THE LADDER

*   *   *

Resting the ladder against the wall, I think
of the people who did this before, stripping
layer after layer of wallpaper in all colours,
none that we like. Magenta, dark green, purple,
soon to be brilliant white. These strange patterns
suited someone and cling, despite polycell
and water, to the knobbly walls where we
will acknowledge their permanence with a layer of woodchip
concealing many sins. I shall be glad, though, that when
we have it as we like it, there will still be ridges
here, bumps there, to impose remembrance.

The earliest plans show *Woodend* at the end of a wood
as now. Our outhouses were the farm, its water
ran from a spring through the cattle-trough to the kitchen.
There are tales of courtship between our farm and the next,
the bridge below being a meeting place for lovers,
sheltered as now in ancient hawthorns.
And every winter, when snowdrifts shape themselves
again to the long-lasting land, we remember that woman
who was found frozen at the ford, her husband at war,
the baby dead up here where she'd left him in safety.

Strangers drive by on the far hill ridge,
going somewhere else. For them, it is just
part of the landscape, another grey farm
with hens, horses, and a lack of trees.
They will scarcely see yet the trees we planted.
A partial metamorphosis of last night's map.
Places we pass through: someone else's destination.

The ladder sways. 'We must buy a new one,'
I remind you, as we pause for coffee.
Three dogs watch our every move. The cat
whose world this is—she was born here—dozes
on my cookery books, contented in the sun.

127

This is no-date, this is just life, life
as usual, as always. You are grey
with plaster-dust, and Tim writes your name
on your forehead. Now we know who you are.
The sun's moved round a little. Time to get on?

*   *   *

Someone who knew what dwelling means
worked out the pattern of these rooms.
We see from our cramped windows
what was first ruled on paper
by no one, a landscape
ancient, not old, and like
the rooms themselves, haphazard
and permanent, the mind
that might have created
not too evident: hints which,
beyond reason, we must
take comfort in loving.
From the moors, the dust
of summer, the snow of winter,
colour the fields yearly afresh,
the stream empties and fills
from beyond our farthest walks.
We feel welcome. This place
is unplanned for us, unlimited
by what we might have imagined.
Like us, someone stopped
on the hill ridge, and said
'here' for his few years' living.
Those who settled, with all that
that means, are dead or moved on.
Over the hill, the council estate
is laid out, dead to the world,
with views determined pen to paper,
even the trees well-planned.
The real people who live there,
our neighbours, walk this way

128

though there is no public right,
to raid the bushes and the stream
whose tiny illegal trout
come to fingers patient with memories.
Their children play with ours,
we learn from them the lie of our land,
in summer we will walk to pubs
at Midhope and Langsett together.
Watching, this first year, the swallow
change to a silent icicle
over the stable door,
and knowing this will be the view
of my old age, I warn myself
we shall never own this place outright.
Not only those who lived here,
but those who cross our space, seem to be
voices and figures that will supplant us.
Through them we talk with the future
which does not listen. Instead,
we listen, already we begin to listen.

Pencil drawing by Sybil

OPEN WAYS
Woodend, September, 1981

1 September — Open Ways

My father would ask me to say
why that sketch is the best
in which the line trails off into infinity
round an unfinished figure.

Underwater, against-the-light magic
of indiscernible forms.
Thoughts, too, wavering away
past the edges of perception.

Night-light, such as the Milky-way
blurs our telescopes with. Expansion,
that places the limit of it all
beyond sight, still travelling outward.

These, life-like, are open ways,
the balance of someone in mid-stride.
When the year tips towards autumn,
buds are beginning again.

Friends, we sit looking out
on the flow of the still fields
gold with stiff corn, brown with ploughing,
the clouds bruised and bright.

Our various lives, unfinished,
make an inner landscape.
Words dart here and there
between us, in a long twilight.

3 September — Braille

The unique self, the unique moment
again and again, irreplaceable,
but born anew. He peels back
the rooty sludge he came up

coated with. I am much
too big for him, he misses
the huge watching shadow,
sees only the still grasses,

the silver meniscus flecked
with tiny flies. His eyes
bob down in the pointed skull,
rise again, glowing wet, big

with life. His fingers are shifting
over the stone, translucent, thoughtful,
like an old woman's hand on the arm
of her chair. I notice the gold

dust expanding on his skin
as he breathes. His mouth opens
on a croak that is gritty
as a puff of pollen. Stiller

than I know how, he collects himself
in the wind's ripples, his life
longer than death could ever be.
I used to think the same of my mother,

half-sleeping in the sun, her fingers
restless enough to pick up the sense
of being from the chair's braille.
Disgustingly vulnerable and beloved.

7 September — Ready to Leave

Ready to leave, you suddenly talk
about the coming disaster. I notice
that the cucumber's tendrils have taken
another hitch, in these last moments.

How, my friend, should we hold in our minds
such oppositions? Young, our shock was to know

131

of the sun's explosion. Unemployed at fifty,
and writing poems, your generous anger

is for these young, more closely threatened,
who lock their despair into fume-filled cars,
make suicide pacts with illicit lovers,
burn themselves, after tea, on the back lawn,

plunge the carving knife to the inward pain.
Premature signs, perhaps, that the final
four-minute warning, already too late
when it will be given, is too awful to wait for.

I think the last day will be like the others,
the wonders of life, about to be dissolved,
already dissolved in our poor attention,
the truth unsaid because fashion forbids.

What duty can we, meantime, fulfill
other than that which has always been ours?
To grow with such persistent angry will
that what is to be killed is worth dying for?

8 September — On the Turn

Blurring pale on the turn, pulsing
against the tide, fanning low
over the grasses then swept away
suddenly to trace an invisible air-stream,

now blurring, pulsing, fanning again,
restless, over the sloping meadows, hour
after hour, with sharp cries but no longer
trilling to claim our land as home.

A bloom of mist has layered the woods.
In shadow the grass-blades retain a glow
of mid-morning dew. The loosened seeds
powder up under the swallows' wings.

132

Watching, I have stood so still that one
hovers inches from me: I am a tree
that might harbour moths or midges.
Forty line up together on the new fence,

preening, flashing a buff underwing,
folding into black seeds streamlined
by the warm south wind they face into,
guessing at the time to go. Not long,

then, before we shall be picking the green
tomatoes, drying the nasturtium pods,
getting out the gumboots, preparing again
for another climate, the swirl not of sand

but snow. A swallow takes off once more
and that throbbing curve to the spread tail feathers,
tense as a bee-sting, as a leaping fish,
amazes as he hovers over a last few meadow-moths.

9 September – Divided

Spinning to the east, the grasses rise
against the glow, the trees are fringed
with burning, the long bulge of moorland,
divided by man, darkens again into one.

The old magic of a sun fallen away
into the earth—its light over other horizons
swelling through haze, gnawing at mountains,
dragging free of scrubland onto a flat sky.

Other bodies are lifted on the earth's bulge
to be warmed once again, while we are drawn
down on the far side, rooted to the spot
almost like any other more fixed thing—

like plants, like beasts, adapted to
wherever life finds us. Even our minds

adopt the local, the temporary, find truth
and love in what and whoever chance offers.

How other, then, all of us might be!
Even as I love this place, I detect
deserts in its grasses, jungles over the moor,
permafrost where the clay lies two feet under.

Unknown languages fret my thoughts
with alien difference, with intimate emptiness.
What names shall I give the familiar sights?
What habits do you expect of me, neighbours?

In the half-light stands my other self,
ready to kill the stranger. I see his body
wrinkle my horizon. Friend, meet me here
where we are both strangers and at home.

10 September — Signs

The fields have been stripped, the hay baled,
but the grass, silkily green again,
hasn't yet stopped growing. Our gold bars
stored in the barns are still bright,

close to, with unfaded flowers. A pile
of nettles I left for the compost crawls red
with escaping ladybirds. A late broody
fluffs her sharp breast over my palm,

lifted from addled eggs. The mealy debris
of the winter wood, which we stacked
yesterday under cover, smells of sap.
Some logs are sprouting fresh leaves.

The signs are mixed, as the feelings are.
Settling the papery hyacinth bulbs in fibre,
I hope darkness will do the trick as usual,
the spikes be firm and full before Christmas.

134

It is good to know we can't do everything,
and have done what we can. The farm feels full,
solid with what may sustain it. The animals
are fat enough to withstand the coming cold.

Next year prepares in the borders the gloss
of crimson tulips, the mist of myosotis,
the purple crispness of the lilac's panicles,
the michaelmas daisies' white reminder.

We can and have to do nothing more.
The stab of splinters, the nettle's prickle,
the hay-fever sneeze will become the composite memory
of this and earlier and foreseen harvests.

14 September — Memories

He squinted, as if to see his memories
more clearly against the bright interference
of his garden-centre yard. His plimsoled feet
were restless. Down past the church, in his boyhood,

the cows and bulls, the shires, the pigs,
the sheep and goats would be walked in
from the villages to the big old ground
behind the town hall, now covered in houses.

His gladioli, too, would have stood unspoiled
in the show tents, if only that earlier
date had been kept to. Storm-broken beauty,
spikes flaring crimson-white, vouched for him.

Now they rise up behind my eyes all day
as new fathers and sons vie for pre-war prizes.
The fowl are spotless in their crowing rows,
udders are sponged and talcumed, bulls' curls

brushed up crisply on shoulder and thigh,
coloured wools worked in the stiff tails

135

and spiked manes of the shimmering shires.
We are building up our own depth

of memories. Exchanging comparisons with friends—
last year, the year before, the year
before that—we avoid others whose antics
confirm a neighbourly enmity. Signs

of settling, it seems, cannot all be good.
Along with those marbled flares, I remember
his twice-repeated comment: that he liked
to see plenty of entries, whether good or bad.

15 September — About the Church

Circled about the church, horsechestnuts hang cool
in their own shade, and at noon the steps
pearl with moisture. Tablets of stone,
askew and upright, weather even here

on their windward side: the names are effaced
haphazardly, as angles and paths determine.
Soon Brownies will befriend it. For now,
the churchyard teems with more natural neglect.

Still in flower, the loosestrife has long pods
unravelling cotton-white to a spray of seeds.
Twisting, a diseased sapling grows muscular.
This year's slabs lie grassy among the monuments.

Few have bouquets, even their first September,
though most names here take living shapes
in the shops and offices, on the hill farms.
Such a place is cut across fibres

of continuous time. Follow any one
tombstone, it will lead through ancestral crowds
into millions—beyond civilized man, and Man,
to wordless creatures, down to the persistent

minute beings whose efforts created us.
Vegetation, too, has its ancient history,
its unchronicled struggles, its baffled instincts.
The broken fibres are bleeding a memorial mould.

Craneflies and midges, in the filtered light,
make a brilliant, zigzag dust. Of this parish
now, I wonder how far back the dead
might recognize their only lives in mine.

17 September — Double Light

At five, we're out too early. In an overcast dawn,
only a finger distinguishes the tightest buds
of these mushrooms from daisies: firm, slippery,
a secretive cluster in the cropped grass.

Inquisitive, the horses come up snorting,
dewy, but warm under their tangled manes.
The cats are with us, they flit to and fro
among tussocks which the moon still whitens.

Voices to each other, we call discoveries
in the double light. I turn up my jersey
over a row of buds, but keep in hand
a few with more fragile gills, the best.

Someone must be picking too small, not trusting
to getting here before us. We have to pick,
hustled by him, smaller than we'd wish,
resenting not the trespass but that unmannerly

lack of restraint. Our anger harshens
our own exchanges, as we cover the ground
between us, disagreeing about how small
is too small, relieved when we meet to see

we have chosen the same—words and actions
imperfectly matched across the gap between us.

What reason might justify, the hand refuses,
reluctant to tear too tight a bud from the soil.

Soon, we will both be at work. Meanwhile,
there is time for walking through the dawn chorus,
talking of a future we may well be robbed of.
With no way of knowing, still we'll take our time.

Woodend, seen through the clump of trees on the skyline
Taken by Anne, Winter 1981

*   *   *

The black spaces grow vaster
between each galaxy and the next.
Our sun bobs across
a tightening spiral arm,
drawn into the whirlpool.

What can thoughts clasp
but their own matter, finding
the rise of life there,
what made it, what it will become.
Self just one configuration.

Beyond any disaster—the atom
destroyed and destroying—some further
genesis? Like a child clasping
a tree, I greet the rise
of my life outliving me.

No choice. But the mind rejoices
in choosing, as if its joy
might comfort the cosmos!
Like light passing through a vacuum
that baffles all human sound.